Sirshree

How to attain the complete aim of life

SELF ENCOUNTER
By **Sirshree** Tejparkhi

Copyright © Tejgyan Global Foundation

All Rights Reserved 2005

Tejgyan Global Foundation is a charitable organization with its headquarters in Pune, India.

ISBN : 978-81-84152-82-1

Published by WOW Publishings Pvt. Ltd., India

First edition published in February 2005

First reprint published in January 2023

Printed and bound by Trinity Academy, Pune, INDIA

This book is the translation of the Hindi book titled "Sampurna Lakshya" by Sirshree Tejparkhi.

Copyright and publishing rights are vested exclusively with WOW Publishings Pvt. Ltd. This book is sold subject to the condition that it shall not by way of trade or otherwise, be lent, resold, hired out, or otherwise circulated without the publisher's prior written consent in any form of binding or cover other than that in which it is published and without a similar condition including this condition being imposed on the subsequent purchaser and without limiting the rights under copyright reserved above, no part of this publication may be reproduced, stored in or introduced into a retrieval system, or transmitted, in any form, or by any means, electronic, mechanical, photocopying, recording or otherwise, without the prior written permission of both the copyright owner and the above-mentioned publisher of this book. Any person who does any unauthorized act in relation to this publication may be liable to criminal prosecution and civil claims for damages.

Although the author and publisher have made every effort to ensure accuracy of content in this book, they hereby disclaim any liability to any party for any loss, damage, or disruption caused by errors or omissions, resulting from negligence, accident, or any other cause. Readers are advised to take full responsibility to exercise discretion in understanding and applying the content of this book.

CONTENTS

Preface   7

Part 1   Introduction

Chapter	1.	Self Encounter For A Complete Aim	11
Chapter	2.	The Complete Aim	13
Chapter	3.	Self Encounter	15
Chapter	4.	Snakes Into Ladders	17

Part 2   Transformation

Chapter	5.	No Transformation Without Direction	21
Chapter	6.	The Aim Achievement Triad	23
Chapter	7.	On Your Mark . . . Aim High, Reach Higher	27
Chapter	8.	Get Set . . . Taking Responsibility for Your Aim	29
Chapter	9.	Get Set . . . Smaller Virtues Lead to Success	32
Chapter	10.	Go . . . Know the Law of Creation for Transformation	34
Chapter	11.	The 30 Maxims For Transformation	37

Part 3   Physical Transformation: Encounter with the Body

Chapter	12.	If Health is the Question, ANSWER is the Answer	57
Chapter	13.	Air	59
Chapter	14.	Nutrition	61
Chapter	15.	Sunlight	65
Chapter	16.	Water	66
Chapter	17.	Exercise	68
Chapter	18.	Relaxation	70

| Chapter 19. | Health and Ayurveda | 73 |
| Chapter 20. | Laziness: The Biggest Signpost Of An Untrained Body | 90 |

Part 4 Mental Transformation: Encounter with the Mind

Chapter 21.	The Three Devils	97
Chapter 22.	Three Steps That Will Weaken the Roots of Fear	99
Chapter 23.	Three Steps That Will Topple the Tree of Fear	102
Chapter 24.	The Fear Liberation Mantra	108
Chapter 25.	The One Hour Worry Cure Technique	111
Chapter 26.	Desensitize Yourself from Worry	114
Chapter 27.	Three Questions to Annihilate Worry	116
Chapter 28.	The Law of Averages Wrecks Worry and Destroys Delusion	119
Chapter 29.	Learn to Laugh At Your Worries	121
Chapter 30.	The Problem That Is Not Grave Enough To Slay Me Can Only Strengthen Me	123
Chapter 31.	Twelve Ways to Get Rid of Anger	127
Chapter 32.	Mind Power and Concentration Meditations	135

Part 5 Financial Transformation: Encounter with the Intellect

Chapter 33.	Misconceptions about Money	147
Chapter 34.	The Secret of Financial Growth	153
Chapter 35.	Twelve Prosperity Secrets	160
Chapter 36.	Your Career— The Cornerstone for Financial Success	168

Part 6 Social Transformation: Encounter with the Heart

Chapter 37.	Three Magical Steps Towards Good Human Relations	193
Chapter 38.	The Seven Levels of Relationships	203
Chapter 39.	Accepting— The Cornerstone of Relationships	208
Chapter 40.	The Golden Rule	211

Part 7 Spiritual Transformation: Encounter with the Self

Chapter 41.	The Aim of Spirituality is Happiness	217
Chapter 42.	Open Up and Blossom in Life	221
Chapter 43.	The Quality of Your Life is Governed by the Quality of Your Questions	224
Chapter 44.	Shatter the Framework of Your World	226
Chapter 45.	The Whole Sole Purpose of Your Life	228
Chapter 46.	Self Enquiry	230
Chapter 47.	Spiritual Transformation and Beyond… 12 Steps and 12 States	236
Chapter 48.	Summing it up … Self Transformation is the Transformation of the Self	245
	Appendices	247

Preface

It is absolutely essential to decide your aim in life, because once you do, your priorities change and your present is transformed along with your future.

Do you give enough attention to your health? Are you able to save money for a rainy day? Are you consistent in providing for your loved ones? Are you able to manage your time? Do you work well with others?

Not everyone can answer "yes" to all these questions, but it doesn't have to be that way. You see, the moment you decide on your aim and commit to it, you will see how easy it is to give the time and attention to these things. In fact, your life will take a positive turn as soon as you have identified your aim. So, are you prepared to turn your life around? If your answer is "yes," then please do continue reading this book, *Self Encounter*. It has the power to change your life completely.

This book is divided into seven parts. Each part deals with a particular aspect of life. Part 1 introduces the idea of Complete Aim. Part 2 talks about the Complete Aim as the first step to a complete life. Part 3 is a guide to improving the body's health. Part 4 helps you achieve mental transformation through the improvement of mind power and concentration after learning to manage fear, worry, and anger. Part 5 enlightens and gives a concrete direction to attain financial prosperity. Part 6 helps to improve your social life and teaches you to be comfortable with people and to inspire them. Lastly, Part 7 tackles the myths of spirituality and prepares you to achieve complete spiritual transformation. The VCD accompanying this book will help to make the entire subject more clear.

Altogether, the seven parts of Self Encounter give you the means to realize the Complete Aim, the attainment of which signifies a state where your inner world is no different from your outer world; where your outer world is an expression of your inner world; where you effortlessly influence and leave a lasting impression on those around you; where people love you and cherish you for who you are and as you are since you too love them unconditionally.

To conclude this introduction, remember that the world likes those who are whole and perfect, those who are deceit-free and honest. Such people alone are the true heroes of the future. When they begin to lead a complete life, the world begins to transform.

Part 1

Introduction

Self Encounter for A Complete Aim

This book shall hold a mirror against your growth in all five aspects of life—physical, mental, social, financial, and spiritual. It shall make sure that you do away with the lingering patterns, cycles, and fatal flaws that hinder your growth in these five aspects. It shall make you dive deep into yourself to discover the leader and the communicator within you.

But realize that this is not a mere book. This is a mirror. It is a mirror that you hold before yourself to experience self encounter. The word "encounter" has more than one meaning. For example, it means contending against an opponent in a sport or battle, it also means meeting someone as if by accident. However, for our purposes, it shall pertain to a deeper level of knowing oneself through experience. That is why this book is called *Self Encounter*. In it, you will encounter yourself and see what needs fixing in your life.

To understand this book, you need to know how it has been written. It is actually a compilation of various discourses imparted by Sirshree, a living master. Sirshree's discourses cut through veils of ignorance and make you look at who you really are like in a mirror. They make you laugh; they make you cry—they make you sit up and take notice. But most importantly, they change and transform you. Thousands of seekers—professionals, executives, students, as well as housewives—are now benefiting from his unique, insightful, and highly practical teachings, that help them to enhance the level of love, joy, all-round growth, and success in their lives.

The Complete Aim

An individual may have many aims and gets joy and satisfaction by achieving them. However, he may not be aware that hidden behind every aim is the aim of living a complete life, which is embodied in Complete Aim. This aim beyond all aims is the realization and expression of one's potential.

Complete Aim is achieved first through Self Liberation, followed by Self Development, and then by Self Expression. Self Liberation refers to freedom from negativity which breeds emotions like fear, worry, and anger. Self Development refers to enhancement of positive qualities that work on every level of one's life. Lastly, Self Expression refers to demonstrable results in one's life and that of others after liberation from negativity and development of positive qualities.

Complete Aim = Self Liberation (from problems) + Self Development (in all five aspects of life) + Self Expression (the impact on your life and the lives of others). Aiming step by step towards all three is what makes the aim of one's life complete. This is Complete Aim.

Attainment of Complete Aim is akin to the blossoming of a flower from a little bud. It is similar to a photograph that cannot be seen if there is no output from the camera that holds it. Indeed, for a picture to be appreciated by the world, it first needs to be processed and then printed or uploaded. Likewise is the attainment of Complete Aim. There is a process that needs to be carried out before the final product is revealed.

The one who focuses on Complete Aim is like a warrior who takes every challenge in life head on; responding promptly to adversities without complaint or regret. To most people, approval in the eyes of others is what counts, but what matters most to such a warrior is the commitment to living a complete life.

Hence, such a warrior is one who has clarity in body, mind, and intellect. Clarity with respect to the body refers to being aware of the nature of the body—its breath, the interplay of the physical elements within it, its need for adequate food and sleep, and its requirements to remain healthy. Clarity with respect to the mind refers to clarity of thoughts, emotions, and various other mental states, of not getting caught up in mental turbulence, and staying clear and balanced amidst the barrage of random thoughts and varying situations. Clarity of intellect refers to not being muddled or confused about what is happening in one's life.

A person who has clarity at the intellectual and experiential levels is a warrior who has encountered his own self.

3

SELF ENCOUNTER

As mentioned in the first chapter, the word "encounter" by itself can mean many things. In this book, you will be working with only one kind of encounter—Self Encounter, which is knowing oneself experientially at the deeper levels. In its most basic form, knowledge could be interpreted as an individual's experience through words—written and spoken. In other words, it is an expression of the intellect. But experiential knowledge is what is more important, and it goes beyond intellectual knowledge.

Let's assume that you are told the deepest secret of the universe. Will you be able to understand the meaning behind the words? What if you are given a book to read about the subject? Will then the universe be more comprehensible? The words would seem to be empty until you experience the meaning behind them. Understand that Complete Aim is the one aim that transforms the three layers of an individual—the body, mind, and intellect, as well as the five aspects of one's life—the physical, mental, social, financial, and spiritual. But mere understanding is not enough.

For transformation of the body, you must exercise, maintain a proper diet (a pure diet), get timely and adequate rest, and practise breath control *(pranayam)*. Also, you should take advantage of all the gifts of nature such as air, water, sunlight, natural herbs, etc. You must realize that although many have deep knowledge about the body, only when they practise what they know, do they truly encounter their body.

For transformation of the mind, you should practise cultivating happy and optimistic thoughts while holding a strong aim. Be deeply watchful of your thoughts and you will be liberated from vices and debilitating emotions such as fear, worry, anger, and the like. The mind can have loads of information, but only when one puts it into practise does one truly encounter the mind.

For transformation of the intellect, you should practise farsightedness, originality, practicality, efficiency, and giving the required response to any situation. Many people think they understand the intellect, but only when they practise what they understand, do they truly encounter their intellect.

There are action plans at the end of each section of this book to help you encounter yourself. As you progress through each section, you can plan your actions on those pages, and then bring your plan into action. By doing so, you will have what we call *knowlerience*—or knowledge and the experience together—of self transformation. With knowlerience, you would be capable of turning your snakes into ladders.

4

SNAKES INTO LADDERS

In the classical board game of snakes and ladders, you progress up the ladders and slide down on the snakes. Self transformation becomes easy if you have learned to turn every snake into a ladder and thus can always climb up in life. As you practice the guidelines given in this book, you may encounter some obstacles along the way. Do not let these obstacles become excuses. Transform every obstacle into an instrument for growth. These are your snakes to be turned into ladders.

One obstacle could be your inability to devote enough time and energy to finish reading this book. To counter that and turn the snake into a ladder, you can reason (truthfully) with yourself that reading this book regularly will help to improve your concentration and focus. Another possible obstacle could be that you may find it hard to understand some of the contents of this book. Just remember that persistence and patience make for progress, and you will hurdle this obstacle despite all odds! You simply have to read some chapters more than once. Read and reread until you grasp the meaning beyond the words. It's as simple as that. Still another obstacle could be that you may not have a teacher to guide you along your journey. In that case, form a study group and work on the practices together in the pursuit of knowlerience and self-transformation.

***

For many people, life is a series of problems. It's these people who fail to see that life gives the greatest opportunity to attain the everlasting bliss of self-realization. Are you one of them, or are you someone who already has a glimmering of realization that leads to self-realization?

With this book, Self Encounter, in your hands, the doorway to self-realization is opened. From the beginning up to the final part on spirituality, the process of self-development through self-realization as revealed in this book will lead to true self-transformation. It is up to you to take up on it and reap the benefits in your life.

This book has been compiled from Sirshree's teachings by selecting extracts from his many discourses about life in which he teaches the art of transforming snakes into ladders.

Part 2

Transformation

5

NO TRANSFORMATION WITHOUT DIRECTION

Those who strive to accomplish their aim in life are the Resolute. Your first step to be one of the Resolute is to develop a goal and be the bearer of an aim. You must be like an archer gauging a target and concerned only in setting his sight to hit the mark. When you become as focused as an archer who sees nothing else but the target, you become a Resolute.

Many examples of people who have become Resolute can be cited. For instance, there are several stories of women who have lost their entire family in accidents except for a child. Naturally, they become depressed and some even contemplate suicide. But then they look at their child and remember that they have the responsibility and the desire to care for them. With an aim defined for them, they are able to conquer their sorrow. Thus, a definite aim can give meaning and direction to your life and it also helps to overcome any problem, psychological or otherwise, with ease.

Life has many distractions. Unless we are mindful of our aim, we become oblivious to any purpose except for our routine duties. Have you identified your aim in life yet? If your answer is no, then isn't it about time to zero in on your aim and work towards it as best as you can? If you already have an aim, then why not breathe life into it? With a clear aim, your life has meaning and no obstacle would be too big to handle. Without a clear aim, trivial problems appear huge and you may feel as if the world is closing in on you at the slightest of inconveniences. Have you ever experienced going ballistic one morning at work after you got served a cup of coffee that's already cold, or had cream when you specifically instructed your coffee to be black? Without an aim, little things like that can make you act a bit crazy—if not totally crazy. With a clear aim, even the greatest slips in life won't be a bother to you at all.

So strengthen your life with the right aim. Help life to help you. Don't wait for opportunities to come to you. Don't wait for people to come your way to remind you of your aim in life. It's likely they will never come. Your aim is for you to know. It's what will give you direction, so go find it. It will be a golden day indeed when you are able to find an aim for your life.

THE AIM ACHIEVEMENT TRIAD

Everyone has the desire to succeed in life, yet most people are not prepared for the change they want to happen. Many dream of becoming a millionaire, or even a billionaire, but are often not prepared to efficiently handle that kind of wealth. People normally yearn for the ultimate but many are not ready to receive it.

Are you truly prepared to receive what you're praying for? Do you think you're prepared for a total self-transformation? Have your efforts shaped you enough to be the heir to a royal life? When you are totally prepared to accomplish something, then you naturally draw that thing towards you. But in order to get prepared, you need to take sure steps, which is what The Aim Achievement Triad provides.

The Aim Achievement Triad is the definitive 3-step guide towards one's aim.

(1) Decide your aim (On your mark...)

(2) Prepare for your aim (Get set...)

(3) Plan your work and work your plan (Go)

These three vertices of the Aim Achievement Triad encapsulate the foundation of total self-transformation. The first node in the triangle is where an aim is chosen and accepted. This initial step is where you define an aim which sets your life in the right direction.

The second node is about discipline and preparation to reach your aim. To illustrate, consider that out of a hundred people who win the jackpot in the lottery, more than ninety go back to being poor within a year. The cause is none other than a lack of discipline and being unprepared. Once you reach the peak of success, discipline and self-control are the key factors required to stay at the top. Some people may find it easy to climb the ladder of success, but because of lack of discipline, they don't last and eventually fall down from whatever height they have reached. Discipline is all about doing away with undesirable traits like laziness and addictions. It's about developing patience, courage, self-confidence, honesty, and fearlessness among other good traits. It takes discipline to avoid the bad influence of so-called friends who encourage destructive activities involving alcohol, smoking, drugs, gambling, and other vices. Unchecked, these can become habitual and difficult to curb as they play with your senses and trick the brain into submission. Consequently, they become huge stumbling blocks to achieving your aim.

A vital part of the preparatory step towards an aim is achieving discipline in regard to the body's senses relating to the tongue, the eyes, and the hands.

Discipline of the Tongue

Your preparation towards an aim requires a discipline of the tongue, or the practice of proper speech. Those who are not disciplined in speaking fall easy prey to the following six ill manners that hinder progress:

(1) Using harsh, rude, bad, and abusive language

(2) Being sarcastic as a response to someone reproaching you

(3) Lending your opinions even when you are not asked to

(4) Backbiting and inciting quarrels

(5) Indulging in rumour mongering

(6) Speaking without prior thinking

Discipline of the Eyes

The ones who are not disciplined in the use of their eyes fall easy prey to the following six vices of sight and thus hamper their advancement:

(1) Aimless surfing on the internet and television

(2) Watching movies without any limit or restraint

(3) Habitually looking for negative qualities in others

(4) Lustful fantasizing

(5) Reading trash and worthless stories in newspapers, magazines, or the internet

(6) Getting blinded by appearance and wealth over knowledge and wisdom

Discipline of the Hands

Those who are not disciplined in the use of their hands fall easy prey to the following six bad habits regarding work and thus delay their growth:

(1) Finding excuses to avoid work

(2) Being careless

(3) Leaving tasks incomplete

(4) Not observing cleanliness of the body

(5) Interfering in the work of others

(6) Postponing work and not being punctual

The third step of the aim achievement triad involves chalking out a systematic work plan and keeping to it. As was mentioned before, plan your work and work your plan.

Divide the process of achieving your aim into small steps and see how long it would take to complete each one. By breaking up big chores, even the greatest and most difficult task will seem small and easy. A steady and definite work plan can assist you in hitting your target. While there will always be things about the future that will not be clear to you, they are not obstacles to your work plan because a strong willpower always gets you through anything.

Do you realize that by simply thinking "I cannot do it" your plan can get derailed? Be fearless and optimistic. You climb the ladder of success as you learn from your mistakes. Remember that success is born from the womb of failure and there is always a silver lining to every dark cloud. This means there is a hidden boon in every difficulty. You can attain this boon only by staying firmly on the path of your aim.

Giving the right direction to one's life is the need of anyone who longs for self-transformation. The Aim Achievement Triad lends a direction to anyone's life, such that the Resolute who takes up an aim becomes totally disciplined and works unflinchingly on what's planned.

ON YOUR MARK . . .
. . . AIM HIGH, REACH HIGHER

The higher your aim, the greater are the strength and courage that life grants to you. Those who understand such laws of nature are never satisfied with lower aims. If you know that nature is your ally, it makes sense to aim high. The moment you do this, your body, mind, and intellect go on autopilot and you get primed for success. Still, not many make it to identifying their aim in life. Of those who do, few set their sights towards their aim, and of this number, only a handful get to within sight of their aim.

To succeed, it helps to develop a larger than life aim that excites you and makes you happy. Your aim must inspire you to work hard and make you forget your fears. Your aim must be a constant in your mind.

To be mindful of your aim in life, write it down, and don't just do it in your personal diary—write it down and paste it on all those places where you are bound to look time and again. Stick it on the bathroom mirror, your computer, your car's dashboard, your refrigerator, your briefcase, and other items that you use every day.

If you wish to keep it a secret from others, then use abbreviations or symbols that you alone can understand or associate with your aim.

With your aim at hand, ask yourself the following questions:

(1) Is your aim big enough, good enough, and beneficial to others?

(2) How much are you interested in achieving your aim?

(3) What powerful intentions drive your aim?

(4) Is your aim practical enough or are you merely building sand castles in the air?

These questions serve as guidelines to point you in the right direction. They prepare you to face the troubles that can be expected in life. If you are without direction, then your philosophical attitude towards life is something like this: "If there is life, there are problems; if there are problems, there is misery; if there is misery, there can be no joy or peace." This is the vicious cycle of the directionless.

The good news is that there is also a virtuous cycle of the Resolute, and if you belong here, then your attitude towards life is: "Where there is life, there is an aim; where there is an aim, there are the Resolute who turn problems into opportunities by learning from the mistakes that caused the problems; where there is learning, there is growth."

GET SET . . .
TAKING RESPONSIBILITY FOR YOUR AIM

Are you ready to take on responsibilities? Do you know the kind of responsibilities you are prepared to handle? Think of an experience you've had in taking up a certain responsibility. Can you recall how it felt? Being responsible is really a great experience if you take the time to prepare. Remember when you took up the responsibility of studying hard to get good marks in an exam? Upon getting a high grade, it's natural to experience a sense of fulfilment—something which is cherished by every human being.

If you are overweight, you can take it upon yourself to slim down within a certain time frame. As soon as you take up this challenge, you will experience vigour and a renewed energy within you that weren't there before. You will be surprised at how the very thought of being responsible prepares you for the work required, which by itself is already a great inspiration.

In life, you tend to deal only with those people who are responsible. For instance, would you continue to purchase items from a shopkeeper who keeps promising to deliver goods to your home on time, but always fails to do so? Would you keep friends who say they will do you a favour but fail to follow through, giving you a silly excuse instead? If you prefer not to deal with people who are irresponsible, how can you expect others to trust you if you yourself are not responsible?

Ask yourself about where you are today and of the things you've promised yourself you would do but have never done. Have you taken it upon yourself to be responsible for the things you do and what happens to your life from here on? A lot of people couldn't care less about being responsible for themselves. Let's take being responsible for weight loss as an example. It's a fact that many overweight people out there know that they need to exercise but never get down to it. Many people indulge in vices such as smoking and drinking even when they know very well that they shouldn't. Why is this so? If one is aware of something and yet there's a gap between his intention and action, then it's a sure sign that he is in denial.

Once you take responsibility, it's very easy to be free of any vice. The chain smoker who takes responsibility for his health and decides to give up smoking experiences the kind of joy that's far beyond the fleeting pleasure he used to gain from cigarettes.

Ask yourself what your flaw is and the virtues you need to adopt. You must answer these before you complain about things like a lack of money and how "the system" has failed to support you. Ask what you are responsible for and whether you are fulfilling your responsibility.

Here are a few things in life that you can take responsibility for:

(1) Not indulging in any vice
(2) Earning enough money for your livelihood
(3) Owning your own house

(4) Helping a friend in need

(5) Self transformation

Now that you know the things to be responsible for, you must keep track of what's happening around you and ask yourself how your circumstance fits a responsibility you can handle. The world may seem unfair, but if you only complain about the shortfalls of people, government, and everything else, then, you will get nowhere. You must learn to accept responsibilities now. By being aware of the importance of taking up a responsibility, you will be ready to accept the greatest responsibility of all, which is to know oneself. This is the responsibility that must be accepted by each one of us, if not today, then tomorrow. Once it happens, then self transformation can truly be completed.

9

GET SET . . . SMALLER VIRTUES LEAD TO SUCCESS

There's this saying: "First man develops habits and then it's the habits that develop a man." Did you know that the best habit you can develop is the habit of adopting new good habits? Repetition of old bad habits does not help in any way in your progress.

The following are habits or virtues that must not only be put into practice but should also be improved on day by day till they are mastered. These virtues may not seem to be highly impressive, nevertheless these are the ones that will lead you to success.

(1) **Courage:** The courage to undertake certain calculated risks is helpful in transformation.

(2) **Patience:** The fruits of patience are always sweet. Plan patiently. Execute even more patiently.

(3) **Reflection:** Constantly practise the art of reflection. The habit of refection is the key to happiness.

(4) **Honesty:** Every person admires honesty. Even the dishonest wants others to be honest with them.

(5) **Keeping promises:** Always keep your word. People will respect you if you have made commitments and fulfilled them. Nobody trusts the one who does not keep promises.

(6) **Self-confidence:** Whatever you do, do it with complete confidence and dedication. Self-confidence results in a feeling of faith. It is akin to a life-giving energy. Faith is a great feeling. Let this feeling work for you. Faith and strong willpower help simplify even the most difficult of tasks to a great extent. Accept the challenge of delivering a speech to an audience. Prepare well and deliver it well. Self-confidence will be the automatic result.

(7) **Unyielding faith in God:** Unyielding faith is something that does not shatter under any circumstance. This is trust born out of understanding. Anyone who possesses this kind of trust realizes that God (Universe, Nature) has created him and shall take care of him until the end. Thus, there is strength and faith in his prayers. Faith itself gives him the right guidance and intuition at every moment. If any problem occurs in his life, he does not break down; instead he understands the cause of the problem and, with faith, addresses the cause.

(8) **Fearless eyes:** Be bold and undertake those tasks which you fear. This will gradually put an end to every fear within you. It is foolish to fear failure. Hence, gain knowledge. After having done so, you will realize that success is born from the womb of failure. Every problem has a gift enclosed. If you see dark shadows, then you can be certain that there is light nearby. Else, shadows cannot be formed. The ones with fearless eyes are those who have no fear at all in the face of any problem. It's the problems that get scared and flee from them. Problems do not give the fearless burdens but instead give them pleasant surprises that accompany every solution. Boldness is essential in working towards your complete transformation.

10

GO . . . KNOW THE LAW OF CREATION FOR TRANSFORMATION

The world has three kinds of people. The first are the masters of their life, the second have life as their master, and the third are those who neither rule their life nor are ruled by it. The first are those who are seen as successful and who create and shape the events in their life. The second are the ones perceived as unsuccessful and whose destinies are shaped by others. The third are indifferent and are neither completely successful nor complete failures. They are also not extremely happy or unhappy, although something or the other always troubles them. Do you belong to one of the first two, or do you belong to the third category? Only you can decide as to which category you belong to. But once you understand the power of the law of creation, you can't help but get into the first category.

The law of creation has been in existence since time immemorial and is thus older than humanity. The law is constantly creating something whether we understand it or not and it works in every facet of life. Once you understand this law, you can control it. Otherwise, it controls you.

There are three steps to master the law of creation.

First Step: Understand the Law

The law of creation states that every thought turns into reality. Once you let powerful universal thoughts pass through your mind, the law starts working for you. All that has been divinely created for you begins to overflow in your life—joy, love, abundance, health, right goals, knowledge, wisdom, etc. Through this law, you can find happiness, which will inspire you to spread happiness among others. As you begin caring for the world, your own minor cares and worries disappear. Those who find contentment are the ones who can help others.

Whenever you hear someone say that anything you want can be attracted by thinking positive thoughts, you find it hard to believe. Your mind thinks it can't be that easy. That is why you need to understand the law of creation. The best part of this law is that it works whether you believe it or not. There really is no harm in trying it out.

The law works because the mind is interconnected with the river of Consciousness. All your thoughts constantly pour into this river. This river turns whatever you think into reality. It has unlimited power. The only thing you need to do is to send a continuous stream of thoughts about what you want. You can harness its power because you are by nature complete, perfect, and are connected to Consciousness (God). You do not have everything you seek in life only because you do not continuously think about the thing you desire. Anything you think and believe can be created.

Second Step: Happy Thoughts

Having understood the law, you need to maintain a stream of happy thoughts. Repeat happy thoughts whenever you can. Repeat the thought, "God obeys man only when man obeys God. Man needs God for his energy and God needs man for his expression." Whenever you are sick, instead of thinking negatively, repeat to yourself, "I am sick today because my thoughts are disconnected from the thoughts of the divine; otherwise I am healthy. Henceforth, I will let only divine thoughts pass through my body-mind."

Third Step: Surrendering

In the third step, you must surrender all your thoughts and aspirations to the law of creation. Say in your mind, "The divine thinks rightly through me. These thoughts will manifest in accordance with the law." With this thought, you can get on with your day to day work and leave the rest to the law. Whenever you have a problem and you are in doubt of the law, remind yourself, "I am happy because everything is in the hands of the divine. I am certain that the divine will take care of it."

Further, you can even declare: "I am releasing my thoughts into the universe. The universe does not have the problem of _____ (state your problem). I am no longer affected by the problem. I bow to the universal power which now guides me in every way. I surrender completely to its force."

The three steps mentioned here are tested and proven. The more you elevate yourself through them, the more you forget your own worries and begin to care for others. This is the greatest way to get rid of worry.

It's natural to consider your loved ones to be your only family. But you should know that the whole world is actually your family. Whatever you do to help the world will also benefit you and give you immense happiness. By elevating yourself by means of the law of creation and making others happy, you make yourself happy as well.

30 MAXIMS FOR TRANSFORMATION

To achieve success in anything, you have to finish what you have started. For the impossible to become possible, constant practice is essential because that is what will allow transformation to happen.

Here are 30 maxims for you to reflect on and use to hasten transformation:

(1) Examine Yourself

Each night, before you go to sleep, try to recollect whatever you did earlier. Better still, try to see yourself as you went about your business through the day and relive all that you had done from the time you woke up to the moment you went to bed. If you do this tonight, you will feel heightened awareness tomorrow. In this way, your level of awareness will increase with each passing day. In addition, your memory will also improve.

(2) Develop the Habit of Diary Writing

Write down all upcoming tasks and challenges in your diary.

All your action plans for transformation should be included in a diary which serves as a handy tracking tool. If you wish, you can involve a friend who can review your diary from time to time and give you constructive feedback and motivation.

(3) Recognize Opportunities

Opportunity always knocks at your door but as it usually comes in different guises, you often don't recognize it and shut it out of your life more often than not. You thus miss the chance to accept a blessing. An opportunity may appear to be bad news to you, but the truth is that every problem, doubt, or difficulty is actually opportunity in disguise. As emotions tend to cloud judgment, you do not see opportunities as they are. But by being aware of what knocks at your door, you will be able to recognize opportunities as they come and make the most of what you receive in life.

(4) Obey the Golden Rule

"Do unto others what you want others to do unto you." This is the Golden Rule and it's really very simple to understand, but still, some people find it hard to follow. The Golden Rule has a lot to teach you. You can read more about it in Part 6, Chapter 41.

(5) Develop Decision Making Skills

Learn to take decisions even if they turn out to be wrong at times. Make use of both your head and your heart in decision making but be guided foremost by the heart. Use your head when the heart tells you to. But be aware that there is something greater than the heart and the head, which is the source of all thoughts and feelings known as tejasthan—"the bright place" within you. This is the point where the Universal Self connects with the human body. You can learn how to access the Source effortlessly (this is easily possible in the retreats held by Tej Gyan Foundation, refer to the appendix for further details). Only those who are guided by the Source should guide the world because only they have true wisdom and knowledge.

(6) Choose Your Team

Choose your company wisely. Choose a team which you can work with to help you attain your aim. Who among the people around you harbour happy thoughts? Choose team members or friends who motivate you when you tell them of your big dreams, and not ones who express skepticism and are discouraging to your goal. With a good team, even the most difficult of tasks becomes easy.

(7) Do It Today and Now

What can be done today should not be set aside for tomorrow. Otherwise, up to half of your time the next day will likely be taken up to finish what should have been done the day before. It's always counterproductive to postpone things that can be done right away. At the beginning of the day, decide what all tasks need to be done, then complete those tasks first that you find boring, because you will definitely make time to complete the tasks that interest you. If you manage tasks in this way, you can complete them all. Task management is a great way to stay motivated while at work.

(8) Learn the Art of Completion

Have you ever wondered why your mind is frequently preoccupied by the past or the future? And why is it that some people dream a lot at night? It's because their present is incomplete. Like most people, they may have left many of the tasks of the day unfinished. But as their mind feels troubled by this, their subconscious mind takes over at night while they sleep and completes those tasks for them, even if only in dreams. This phenomenon underscores the importance of task completion. The underlying desire behind the performance of a task or the fulfilment of a responsibility is essentially the same for everyone. It is to experience the feelings of joy and satisfaction—natural emotional rewards for the accomplishment of tasks.

Just like tasks, relationships can also be left incomplete. Did you know there is a process of "completing" with people wherein you tell people how you feel? It is a process of sharing your feelings with others. If you are annoyed with someone for example, it does not help to simply allow yourself to simmer in annoyance, leaving the situation behind without a resolution. You need to "complete the circle" with the other person, you need to communicate and say something like, "I am annoyed because of what you did." The intent here is not to encourage conflict but rather to effect completion and bring balance in the relationship.

Unfortunately, there are some people who tend to take to extremes, and say something infuriating to the other party such as, "Can't you do anything right?" Otherwise, they'd say nothing at all, leaving the situation open-ended and the offending error uncorrected, which encourages repetition or an escalation of negative emotions. Just follow the middle path and permit closure with the other person by gently sharing exactly how you feel rather than seething inside and later wilfully wronging the person in turn like in a game of chess. The Art of Completion is no game. It is a process wherein you complete what has been left undone and wherein you establish completion with everyone else.

(9) Practise Every day

Every singer, artist, magician, and practically every successful person in the world admits that practice is the key to success.

Practice makes man perfect. (Incorrect)

Perfect practice makes man perfect. (Correct)

Think about it. Why is it that people working in a circus are able to walk on a tightrope whereas some people fall down even while walking on a straight wide road? The answer is Perfect Practice. You can master any skill if you do the same thing repeatedly day in and day out, and gradually raise the level of challenge. The key word is gradual. Let's say you want to be a master weightlifter and you begin training with 60 kg. If you lift this weight regularly and increase it by a kilogram every week, you will be surprised at your progress in a few months. In order to move mountains, first learn to lift little stones.

(10) Learn Time Management

Everyone on Earth has the same amount of time, so you should never say, "I don't have time." Time is valuable. The higher your aim, the more you need to learn time management. Done at the proper time, even the smallest work has great value. But any work done after its time has passed loses value, no matter how big it is. If you love your life, you must learn how to manage your time. Time is life, and if you waste time, you also waste your life. If you know how to accomplish any task at the decided time, then you would have learned how to use time properly. Those who postpone work for tomorrow only invite problems to themselves.

(11) Build Your Character

Every person's character can be built if, from time to time, there is cleansing and purification through self-reflection and external inspiration. External inspiration can be experienced by reading the biographies and autobiographies of great personalities. By finding out what great men and women have experienced and accomplished, all your weaknesses can be brought to light to be cleansed out knowing how those great characters have successfully dealt with them. Purify your mind by forgiving yourself for all the wrongs you have done. Get rid of guilt and see how every mistake can be a wise teacher.

(12) Keep Your Mind Clear

Clarity of your mind is essential for self transformation. The practice of yoga and meditation can keep your mind clear and improve your mind power.

(13) Develop the Habit of Reading

Read good books. Read literature that is inspiring. Read religious books like the holy scriptures regularly. Join a library or a reading awareness group. Books can prove to be good friends if chosen carefully. Those who are fond of reading books are not prone to boredom or loneliness. Books can help to develop your knowledge, thinking, and imagination. Readers can be good leaders.

(14) Develop Yourself Using the Power of Imagination

You are what you think you are. Whatever you imagine yourself to be will be made manifest. But be warned that an overactive imagination if not controlled is an invitation to mental problems. But if imagination is disciplined, then it becomes a ladder for progress.

When imagining, always keep your mind open to the highest of ideals. Do not allow your imagination to be poisoned by obscene pictures, vulgar movies, or cheap shows. The imagery and ideas from such programs can pollute your power of imagination. Watch only the things that help you reach your goal.

(15) Try New Experiments

As a child, you may have been fond of experimenting with things, and each time you did so, you may have learned something new in the process. To continue learning, you must always try out new things. The following activities can help you experience the world in new ways and allow you to learn new things.

- Observe total quietness by taking a vow of silence for a day. This is for you to look into your mind clearly and understand the tricks it plays. In the silence, you will be able to talk to and listen to yourself as if for the first time.

- Tie a piece of cloth over your eyes for a day. For your safety, do this with the permission and guidance of family members. With your eyes closed, you will be able to realize and see something which you had never seen before. You will also find yourself being grateful for the gift of sight you have received.

- You can also try other experiments or activities that you haven't done before, such as…
- repairing a broken gadget at home
- drawing a picture
- organizing a certain program
- speaking to strangers

New experiences through experimentation bring new awareness.

(16) Conquer Laziness

Laziness is the greatest hurdle on the path of progress at the body level. To overcome laziness, you can do the following activities:

- Do some daily physical work like yoga, aerobics, weight training, tai-chi, etc.
- Work on a task or two every day which you feel are not essential and can also be done the next day. This will help you in breaking the habit of procrastination.
- See if there's anything else that needs to be done before bedtime. Do it before you sleep.
- Spend some time, energy, and money to learn something new even if your mind isn't willing.
- Meet new people and participate in a local activity even if you have to drag your feet to do it.
- Do social work that could bring some changes in society.
- Attend hobby classes where you can learn a craft like music, dance, art, personality development, memory enhancement, Reiki, and other practices you have heard or read about.

- Write a poem, article, or story for a newspaper, magazine, website, or just for your own satisfaction.
- Compose a letter or email and send it to someone living in a different part of the world.
- Lessen your tendency to watch television or play with your social networking account.
- Consider giving up television, video games, coffee, tea, or any other addictive activity for a month or two.

(17) Destroy the "If Only" Attitude

There are five "if onlys" that many people use as an excuse which keeps them from growing:

- If only I was born in a rich family, I could be more successful.
- If only I had political connections, I would be more successful.
- If only I was born in a big city, I could become more successful.
- If only I was born male instead of female, I'd have more chances of being successful.
- If only my sun sign were different, I'd have better luck.

Break away from this "if only" syndrome and only then you can experience true transformation.

(18) Learn from Life the Way It Teaches You

You should welcome the hurdles and issues of life since they are there to teach you a lesson that is essential for you. Life has its own way of teaching, although sometimes it teaches with a jolt. The ways of life can be strange but you should embrace everything that it has to teach and learn from them.

(19) Set Your Sights on Knowledge

It's only natural that you notice things around you that are flashy and rich, such as fancy cars and sparkling jewellery, and admire the wealth of those who own them. But is it really these things that you need to fix your sights on? No. You need to look deeper beyond the obvious and focus on knowledge and intellect instead of the money one possesses whenever you look at someone. You must understand that every individual can always teach you something new. To learn something from someone else is to be inspired. So if you set your sights on seeking knowledge, then it follows that all that is expected of a successful life will come to you.

Thus, always search for knowledge in others. Do not pay attention to only their physical appearance or wealth. Knowledge is above these things and if you come across a person rich in knowledge and wisdom, consider appointing him as your mentor. He or she can be a guide to set your path more clearly towards your future after which you will begin to find that life is really much easier and simpler than before.

(20) Do Not Fear Criticism

Interact freely with everyone in spite of the fact that there will always be those who will criticize you, close their minds to your ideas, and go on a blaming spree at your expense. To overcome that, all you need to do is to work the best you can and forget that you were criticized at all.

(21) Shun a Mechanical Life

Ninety percent of the people in the world are leading a mechanical life. They behave and act like a machine. If cursed by somebody for example, their automatic response is to reciprocate in kind, repeating and retaliating the same way every time as if programmed to do so. The concept of abuse for abuse or blood for blood simply takes up a greater part of their psyche. These are the people who live and die a mechanical death. When you come to the realization that you have led a mechanical life, you wake up to a renewed one full of love and joy.

(22) Always Be Triumphant

The key to transformation is to always be triumphant. This

can be accomplished if you make sure you never lose to failure. In other words, you must never let your failures to be your fall. If there is fear after your failures, then it heralds your defeat. But failing only means you have lost a battle and not the war. To fail is really just an opportunity to learn from your mistake and move ahead with confidence. All successful people have had to face failures, but they easily overcome each one as they moved ahead by counting their successes. A child falls several times while learning to walk, but he simply gets up again until he learns how to do it right. The ones who do not regret their failures always win. They embrace their failures, learn from them, and then they bury them.

(23) Pray for an Illuminating Spiritual Guide

What is the easiest way to total transformation? It is to pray for an illuminating spiritual guide, or a true master, to come into your life. There is immense strength and power in prayer. And once it is answered with the arrival of a truly illuminating spiritual guide, then you need to keep unconditional and unwavering faith in him or her and to wholeheartedly follow the lead.

(24) Attain Supreme Happiness

Do not try to seek false or second-hand happiness. Rather, seek the kind of happiness that is the greatest of all, which is permanent and divine. (Part 7 explains this in detail).

(25) Engage in Bright Laughter

Do not laugh by making fun of others. Instead, let the laughter come from the bottom of your heart and fill your whole being.

(26) Seek Real Development

Do not seek only money, fame, or luxuries. Try to achieve the highest that is possible for a human being.

(27) Live a Holistic Life

Do not live a fragmented or disconnected life by treating yourself as a mere body or mind, as simply a father or a son, or just another boss or office worker trying to get through the day. Look at your life from a higher perspective and see how you are connected with the totality of things. (See Part 7).

(28) Seek the Supreme Truth Humbly

Do not just seek money, a house, a car, good health, comforts, and the like. While these serve a purpose, they are not the real goals of your life. Instead of seeking money and wallowing in material objects, you should nurture the desire to know the Supreme Truth—which is the real purpose of your life. Never start your journey on the path of truth with an "I know everything" attitude. Rather, begin your journey humbly knowing that you don't know everything.

(29) Prepare to Attain Your Aim

You should steer clear of bad habits including drinking, smoking, gambling, destructive criticism, carelessness, procrastination, and the like. But beyond this, you must also get prepared to attain your aim by taking responsibility for it. (See preceding chapters.)

(30) Develop Yourself through Autosuggestions

The body naturally listens to whatever you say, so it makes sense to give autosuggestions for self-development. Autosuggestions, or giving suggestions to yourself, is easy. You can say this to yourself right now: "I am healthy, aware, and courageous. I can do every work with ease and confidence. Good people are entering my life, and I am recognizing the Truth more and more. Each day, in every way, my mind and body are getting better and better. God's eternal strength is guiding me in every aspect." That's only an example and you can make your own autosuggestions based on your needs. With the help of autosuggestions, it is possible to develop your character and personality in your quest for success and transformation. Follow these steps whenever you give autosuggestions:

- Relax your body. Lie or sit down (whichever you prefer) as you say the autosuggestion.

- Give the autosuggestion in silence and with complete faith and understanding.

- If you wish, you can listen to self-recorded autosuggestions in your own voice.

- State the autosuggestion slowly, imbuing it with love and emotion.

- Before and after giving an autosuggestion, say to yourself, "All my suggestions have a positive effect on my body, mind, and surroundings and I shall immediately experience great results."

An autosuggestion given melodiously with rhythm brings faster results. You can sing it to the tune of a favourite song or to the beat of a memorable musical piece. Practise during the course of the day and you'll be surprised at how useful an autosuggestion is if it's delivered using this technique.

The 30 Maxims Action Plan

(1) Examine yourself

(2) Develop the habit of diary writing

(3) Recognize opportunities

(4) Obey the Golden Rule

(5) Develop decision making skills

(6) Choose your team

(7) Do it today and now

(8) Learn the art of completion

9. Practise every day
   _____
   _____

10. Learn time management
    _____
    _____

11. Build your character
    _____
    _____

12. Keep your mind clear
    _____
    _____

13. Develop the habit of reading
    _____
    _____

14. Develop yourself using the power of imagination
    _____
    _____

15. Try new experiments
    _____
    _____

16. Conquer laziness
    _____
    _____

17. Destroy the 'if only' attitude
    _____
    _____

18. Learn from life the way it teaches you
    _____
    _____

19. Set your sights on knowledge
    _____
    _____

20. Do not fear criticism
    _____
    _____

21. Shun a mechanical life
    _____
    _____

22. Always be triumphant
    _____
    _____

23. Pray for a true spiritual guide
    _____
    _____

24. Attain supreme happiness
    _____
    _____

25. Engage in bright laughter

26. Seek real development

27. Live a holistic life

28. Seek the Supreme Truth humbly

29. Prepare to attain your aim

30. Develop yourself through autosuggestions

The Maxims Action Plan

(1) _____

(2) _____

(3) _____

(4) _____

(5) _____

(6) _____

(7) _____

(8) _____

(9) _____

(10) _____

(11) _____

(12) _____

(13) _____

(14) _____

(15) _____

(16) _____

(17) _____

(18) _____

(19) _____

(20) _____

Part 3

Physical Transformation: Encounter with the Body

12

IF HEALTH IS THE QUESTION, ANSWER IS THE ANSWER

The human body is basically made up of four sheaths: the physical/food sheath, the pranic sheath, the mental sheath, and the causal sheath. The outermost sheath is called the physical or the food sheath because it's build from food that's metabolized by breathing air—oxygen in particular. This external body also needs the mind, intellect, and a few other things to allow it to operate and to reach its full potential. It's five requirements are:

(1) Exercise

(2) Pranayam

(3) Timely rest

(4) Optimum diet

(5) Interesting work for the body-mind mechanism that is neither too much nor too little.

Nature provides us with six resources for life which are not only sustaining but healing as well—as if they are doctors. Once you are aware of them, you can make the most of how they give health and energy to your body.

The six doctors of nature are:

A   Air

N   Nutrition

S   Sunlight

W   Water

E   Exercise

R   Relaxation

The body is an amazing instrument that needs to be taken care of so that it can last and perform to its max. It may take some effort, but making a habit of getting enough air, nutrition, sunlight, water, exercise, and relaxation can do wonders for your body. Just remember, if health is your question, ANSWER is the answer.

13

AIR

Some habits are very useful for your health. If you make a habit of breathing deeply once every hour, for example, your lungs will become stronger and your energy will be renewed every time you do it. But that's not to say that you should be taking deep breaths all the time. What you should do is deep breathing at intervals; while the rest of the time the breathing can be medium – neither too deep nor too shallow. Make a habit of breathing in and out through the nose and not the mouth. Try to be, as far as possible, in a clean and airy environment.

Practice Pranayam or Vowel (a, e, i, o, u) Breathing. Pranayam is about controlling your breath for a certain period of time—taking a breath, holding it, and then releasing it. Through pranayam, the energy in the body is cleansed and purified.

Before you lift any heavy weight, you first take in a deep breath and hold it as you make the lift, releasing the air only after you've set down the weight. It's natural to do this because it's how you get enough power to be able to lift a heavy object for a time. In the same way when climbing a flight of stairs, your endurance improves if you take in a long breath before you take the first step up. Those who are able to understand the power of breathing with the first "doctor"—air, and use it properly, can extract more work from their bodies.

14

NUTRITION

Nourishing the body in the right manner is the key to a higher level of energy, reduction of fat, a strong immune system, and a healthy appearance. Food also has a deep impact on the mind, therefore, it's good to consume food that's natural and to give up processed food with too much fat, artificial ingredients, and impurities. Always consume nutritious (satvic) food that contributes to the strength of the body and peace of mind.

Eat "living food" like raw vegetables, fruits, and sprouts. You will experience a satiating yet refreshing "lift" after consuming raw vegetables or fruits by themselves or served as a salad. If you steadily increase the intake of living food, that "lift" then becomes a lasting and consistent sensation of well-being within the body, mind, and emotions. This is because the bioelectric and subtle frequencies within the brain, nervous system, and every cell in the body get replenished with life energy. The high nutritional content found in living food helps to achieve and maintain metabolic balance. Life energy is present in whole, organic, raw, plant-based products. This life energy not only nourishes the body, slows the aging process, and boosts the immune system, but also gently strengthens sensory and intuitive perceptions as well.

As the body is cleansed through the consistent and well-balanced consumption of living foods, it begins to function with more efficiency. Additionally, due to less toxins and residual pollution, it is able to perform all its physical and non-physical functions to its optimum level. Thus, a steady balance within the mind and emotions can be enjoyed quite regularly.

The following guidelines can help you achieve good health:

1. Stick to a balanced diet with carbohydrates, proteins, and fats in the right proportions as specified in health standards.
2. Eat meals at regular times. But if you are not hungry, you can eat less food or even skip a meal.
3. If you feel hungry in between meals, you can drink some water, munch on a fruit or vegetable (like a stick of carrot) or simply drink tomato juice.
4. Avoid heavy meals that distend the stomach and leave no space for water and air.
5. Avoid overeating as this leads to indigestion and obesity, which cause health problems.
6. If you'd like to drink water in the middle of a meal, then sip only a minimal amount.
7. Fast at least once a month to allow the intestines to rest.
8. You can pray for you and your family's good health while preparing food for them.
9. Avoid thinking about problems while eating.
10. Contemplate or meditate on the food you are about to eat.

This is beneficial to keep your mind free of distractions and to increase the secretion of saliva for better digestion.

(a) Close your eyes and smell the aroma of your food.

(b) Open your eyes and look at the food; note its colours and appearance.

(c) Feel and touch the food (if feasible).

(d) Try to imagine the taste of the food when it would touch your tongue, and then start eating it.

More specific guidelines regarding diet:

(1) Avoid excessively spicy food.

(2) Eat raw vegetables and fruits such as carrot, apple, orange, radish, cucumber, pomegranate, beetroot, etc.

(3) Consume more of sprouts, green vegetables, and foods rich in fibre.

(4) Make seasonal fruits a part of your diet. You can eat fruits before or in between meals. If you prefer to eat fruits after lunch or dinner, then serve yourself a little less food to give room to them and maximize the benefits from their nutrients.

(5) Avoid or minimize consumption of tea, coffee, carbonated drinks, and other stimulants. Instead, you can take healthy drinks such as herbal tea, buttermilk, and milk that's been given just one boil.

(6) Avoid the consumption of tobacco, alcohol, and other drugs.

(7) Avoid ice cream, chocolate, foods that contain too much sugar such as jams, jellies, marmalades, and foods with loads of empty calories like sodas and candies.

(8) Avoid junk food, canned food, preserved food, stale food, pickles, non-vegetarian food, and deep fried food. Always consume food that's fresh. Steamed food is healthier than fried food.

(9) Unpolished rice is a healthier option to polished rice. Avoid eating fine flour products and use flour that has choker or course particles of the grains.

(10) Improve your eating habits instead of going on restrictive diets. Always remember that what you eat and drink has a direct impact on how you look, feel, and perform.

The rules of nutrition are simple. Avoid feasting and practise fasting. Stop eating "dead" and heavy food. Start eating food that's "living" and fresh. Pray before meals and stop worrying during eating.

SUNLIGHT

Sunlight is very important for our body and bones as it helps in the natural production of vitamin D which supports the health of our skeletal system.

Sunbathing is a simple way to maintain a normal amount of vitamin D in your body. Cover your face and head, and give a sunbath to the exposed parts of your body. Take this sunbath in the early morning when the rays of the sun are not harsh. Morning sunlight is the best for the body and you can sunbathe either in your backyard or the terrace. But keep your head and face covered with a wet towel to keep the eyes damp and comfortably cool. Do not sunbathe under the scorching heat of the midmorning or afternoon sun and risk dehydration, sunburn, sunstroke, or migraines.

Drink a glass of water before leaving your home in the heat of the afternoon. Do not drink water immediately on returning indoors if you have been out in the sun. This is essential in order to avoid an abrupt change in the body's temperature, which can be harmful.

WATER

We all know the importance of water to clean our body externally, but it is also important to clean the body internally, or from the inside. Drinking ordinary potable water helps clean the digestive tract, urinary tract, skin, and blood of toxins that can cause a number of ailments.

Recommendations on the use of water:

(1) Consume the maximum amount of water daily.

(2) Drink a glass of water on an empty stomach every morning. This is the easiest cure for stomach ailments. You can start with just half a glass of water and gradually increase the amount of water to three glasses. After drinking, do not eat or drink anything for 45 minutes. Water therapy is useful in the treatment of a lot of diseases but you should consider having easy access to a bathroom or privy to urinate when needed.

(3) Wash your eyes several times with clean water on a daily

basis. This will prevent burning and watering and also refresh your eyes.

(4) Besides drinking water, watching it flow also helps keep the mind cheerful.

(5) It is more beneficial to do pranayam on the banks of a river or wherever nature and fresh air are in abundance.

17

EXERCISE

Exercise plays a major role in keeping you fit. It is essential to elevate the body's energy level, build muscles, strengthen cartilages and bones, increase haemoglobin concentration, decrease fat, increase good cholesterol, improve blood pressure, lower blood sugar level, normalize sleep pattern, and prevent blood clots in blood vessels. Best of all, it makes you look and feel great.

Every part of the body should be exercised by stretching and relaxing. Wherever there is some kind of tension in the body, that part should be stretched and then relaxed. People usually start exercising after they have fallen sick. But if you exercise before you get sick, you will never be sick in the first place.

Yoga is the best form of exercise. There are different asanas or postures for every part of the body. Do them as you need to. You can also exercise your body through some lighter and simpler movements, like in aerobics or dance. Brisk walking is the easiest exercise for everybody. If you really want some long-term benefits with this exercise, you should walk for at least 30-45 minutes, four to five times a week. Alternatively, 30 minutes of rigorous activity, such as jogging, will also do.

Most people don't follow a regular exercise program. If you belong to this category, then it's quite likely that when you do begin exercising, you will be quite tired and your body will ache after a while. That's perfectly normal. It takes a few days for your body to adjust, and when it does, the net result will be renewed energy and vitality. For beginners, start by exercising for about 5-10 minutes three times a day. Then as you build up more endurance, work yourself up to 8-12 minutes twice a day. Eventually you will be able to complete one long workout. There are no precise rules while exercising. Generally, you should feel your muscles working hard, but you must not push yourself to the point where you feel you can no longer keep going for more than a few minutes.

18

RELAXATION

Exercise is essential for the body but so is rest. Sleep and restful relaxation will rejuvenate your body and mind.

Some Relaxation Tips:

About 70 percent of the manifestation of stress and fatigue shows around your eyes. To release the stress, sit down in a comfortable position and directly instruct your eyes with a command such as, "Release the stress that's inside you." Likewise, when you feel tired and wish to take some rest, you can tell your eyes, "Let go of the stress." Your eyes will obey your suggestions, and you will be surprised by how refreshed they feel after some time. You can do this every day for relaxation.

In a similar fashion, you can give suggestions to other parts of your body. Deliver each suggestion slowly, lovingly, and rhythmically. If you give instructions to your whole body such as, "Relax" or, "Release the stress," then the body will follow your suggestions and it will soon be stress free. By giving suggestions to every part of your body, you can relax each part and experience more energy as a result.

Consequently, you will be able to perform more work throughout the day.

Sleep is all about resting your body and mind and about preparing the brain for work the next day. After sleeping soundly, you feel fresh and are prepared to welcome the new day with confidence.

A child, a young adult, and an old person do not require the same length of sleep. A baby can sleep as long as 18-20 hours, but an adult person does not need that much sleep. For some people, sleeping 4-6 hours is enough for a good night's rest. Less but sound sleep can be enough to keep the body fresh. If you do not sleep well or long enough at night, taking a cat nap for about half an hour in your free time during the day is extremely helpful. In fact, with practice, your sleep time can be brought down to 7 or 6 hours without any negative effects—that is, if you live by a solid and true aim to look forward to.

Some recommendations regarding sleep:

(1) Do not rely on sleeping pills, although a light dose can be taken for a few days in case of an illness and if prescribed by a doctor.

(2) Worry is the worst enemy of sleep responsible for spreading sleeplessness in today's world.

(3) Read a book or listen to some light music before sleeping. This can help you get to sleep easily.

(4) Stop worrying and being conscious of the clock while trying to get to sleep. This behaviour tends to keep you awake even more.

(5) A "forced attempt to sleep" is the opposite of "sleep" and only serves to keep sleep at bay.

(6) Stop hating others. Love and let live. This attitude will allow you to sleep peacefully without any issues.

(7) Warm milk may be taken for a good night's sleep.

(8) Pray with love and faith before sleeping.

(9) Caress your pillow gently with love as it can carry you into a sound sleep. You can thank your pillow in the morning.

HEALTH AND AYURVEDA

Ayurveda is a medical science that originated in India and provides the knowledge of all the measures that should be taken for a long and healthy life. According to Ayurveda, there are three main body types with each having specific characteristics and disorders, or faults, called doshas.

(1) Vata dosha

(2) Pitta dosha

(3) Kapha dosha

Every individual possesses one of these doshas, but there can be people with a combination of two or even three doshas.

(1) Vata-pitta dosha

(2) Vata-kapha dosha

(3) Pitta-vata dosha

(4) Pitta-kapha dosha

(5) Kapha-vata dosha

(6) Kapha-pitta dosha

Know Your Body-Mind Mechanism

The characteristics and disorders of the three main body types are described here. If your body has all or almost all the symptoms described under one dosha, then that is your body type. If, for example, your symptoms are a combination of more of kapha and less of vata, then your dosha is kapha-vata. Identification of your dosha is the first step towards a healthy life.

(1) Vata (Ether/Air): Restless, Enthusiastic, Disorderly Body

    (a) Restless and energetic.

    (b) Impatient and hasty.

    (c) Imaginative and talkative.

    (d) Speaks hurriedly.

    (If you are of the above-described nature, then it is very likely that your body type is vata dosha or vata-pitta dosha.)

    (e) Learns easily but forgets easily.

    (f) Enthusiastic and energetic, but also moody, whimsical, and self-willed.

    (g) Irritable and prone to stress and worry due to excess vata dosha.

    (h) Has sleeping difficulties and doesn't sleep soundly.

    (i) Disorderly with no fixed eating, sleeping, and resting schedules.

    (j) Often constipated due to poor digestion as a result of an irregular lifestyle; experiences a bad taste in the mouth.

    (k) Has prominent veins.

- (l) Prone to cramps and spasms of the body.
- (m) Gets anxious very easily with work pressure.
- (n) Has dry and rough skin, hair, and nails.
- (o) Intolerant to the cold season. Hands and feet are usually cold (which is indicative of vata or vata-kapha dosha).

(2) Kapha (Earth/Water): Quiet, Pleasant, Slow Body

- (a) Slow, relaxed, and steady; opposite to vata.
- (b) Doesn't get tensed or angry easily; calm and cool.
- (c) Life is regular and steady.
- (d) Learning ability is slow but has exceptional long-term memory.
- (e) Slow but makes firm decisions.
- (f) Forgiving, loving, pleasant, and tolerant.
- (g) Can't tolerate cold and humid weather.
- (h) Large and firm body type.
- (i) Takes slow but calculated steps while walking.
- (j) A night person – finds it difficult to rise in the morning but can work late into the night. Is energetic for a longer period of time.
- (k) Tendency to gain weight and be fat.
- (l) Slow to digest food.
- (m) Oily, soft, clean skin and clear eyes.
- (n) Thick, black, and curly hair.
- (o) Sleeps deeply; needs eight hours of sleep.
- (p) Can tolerate fasting relatively more than those with vata and pitta dosha.

(q) Prone to asthma, stuffy nose, cough, cold, allergies, and sinus problems.

(r) Has a sweet taste in the mouth; tends to salivate.

(3) Pitta (Fire/Water): Hot, Zealous, Cold-Loving Body

(a) Strong willpower; is therefore assumed to be obstinate by others.

(b) Easily angered but calms down easily.

(c) Capacity to do lots of work.

(d) Has leadership qualities and initiative.

(e) Impatient and meticulous.

(f) Likes to criticize, even himself; hence makes enemies easily.

(g) Accepts challenges easily.

(h) Loves cold weather and cold things like ice cream.

(i) Has a glowing face and skin. If pitta dosha is not controlled, it leads to wrinkles on skin and body odour.

(j) Perspires easily; prone to acne.

(k) Can't tolerate heat.

(l) Palms are hot and sweaty.

(m) Thin, straight, brown hair; tendency to early greying and baldness.

(n) Good digestion; often hungry; can't tolerate fasting; tendency to gluttony.

(o) Tendency for diarrhoea is more than that of constipation.

(p) Spicy food causes chest and stomach burning.

Disease Means Imbalance

Vata: a combination of the elements of air and ether in the body.

It is responsible for the functioning of our body, mind, and senses.

Pitta: a combination of the elements of fire and water in the body. It is responsible for heat, energy, and the digestive power of the body.

Kapha: a combination of the elements of earth and water in the body. It is responsible for the structure of the body and the balance of fluids in the body.

The characteristics of vata are roughness, dryness, and movement. The main characteristic of pitta is heat (fire), and that of kapha is heaviness.

All the three doshas work together to give health and vitality to your body and mind. When all the three doshas are in perfect balance, the body-mind mechanism is healthy. When there is an imbalance between these three, it leads to various physical and mental illnesses. For example, when the vata dosha increases in your body, you experience more roughness in your body, such that your skin and hair become dry and coarse. The internal dryness also leads to constipation, body pains, and a restless mind. When the pitta dosha increases, you experience more heat in the body. When the kapha dosha increases, you experience overbearing heaviness in the body which leads to lethargy, obesity, joint pains, and other things—the details of which are described earlier in this chapter.

The imbalance between the three doshas occurs due to less-than-ideal lifestyles and bad food habits. If you eat in accordance with your dosha or the nature of your body-mind mechanism, you can avoid a lot of ailments. Therefore, it is very important to know your dosha as well as to have the information regarding what foods aggravate a given dosha and what foods are helpful in alleviating it.

Dietary Recommendations and Health Tips

Dietary Recommendations for People of Vata Nature

(1) Food should be hot, soft, fully cooked, heavy, and oily. It should be easily digestible because digestive power is low in vata. Food should be sweet or salty. Avoid bitter, dry, spicy, pungent, cold, and light food. Avoid eating too many food items at a time.

(2) If you are eating sour fruit, add some sugar or salt to it.

(3) Recommended food articles are wheat chapatti, urad dal, moong dal, masoor dal, cow's milk, whey from fresh curds, sweet lassi or buttermilk, ghee, rock candy, ginger, coriander, mint, cumin, caraway, parval, ash gourd, radish, carrot, chaulai, shatavar, beetroot, coconut, dates, grapes, orange (sweet), papaya, ripe mangoes, sweet pomegranate, walnuts, cherries, sweet fruits, almonds, figs, black raisins.

(4) Food articles that should be lessened or avoided are rice, gram, kidney beans, tur, cauliflower, cabbage, peas, raw onion, raw bananas, raw garlic, green vegetables, dry fruits, tea, coffee, alcohol, cigarettes, etc.

(5) Foods that increase vata are mushrooms, spices, sprouts, pomegranates, pears, dry fruits, jowar, bajra, mustard, barley, corn, popcorn.

(6) Soak a few almonds in water at night, remove their skin in the morning, and grind them before eating.

(7) Hot soup taken before a meal also helps in decreasing vata.

(8) A nutritious breakfast is a must.

(9) Avoid fastfood and eat home cooked food. Low calorie, dry, cold food is not ideal for vata people. Food that's not ideal for people with vata may be good for people with kapha.

(10) Use tomatoes and potatoes sparingly.

(11) All types of edible oils are good for people with increased vata but sesame oil is best.

(12) Drink hot milk at night and herbal or ginger tea in the morning.

(13) Use sweet spices like asafoetida, basil, aniseed, cinnamon, and cardamom. These help in improving digestion.

(14) Avoid drinking cold water; instead, take warm or hot water.

Health Tips for People of Vata Nature

Ether + Air = Vata

Symptoms: Shivering, chills, pains, stomach cramps.

Ailments: Gas problems, lower back pain, painful menstrual periods, headache, cracked skin and lips, weight loss, joint pains, low energy.

(1) Avoid late nights as well as staying awake the whole night. Sleeplessness is a sign of vata disorder. Massage head with almond or sesame oil before going to sleep at night.

(2) Take special care of your health in cold and rainy weather.

(3) Avoid too much exercise and stop exercising as soon as you feel fatigue.

(4) Avoid guilt feelings and don't get mired in past mistakes; accept everything and start anew. Forgive yourself and others; love yourself and those around you. These will relieve vata symptoms to a great extent.

(5) Take an enema for constipation—the first step in Ayurveda used for people with vata dosha.

(6) Take a hot water bath in winter. During summer, bathe with warm water. Cold water baths increase the vata and kapha dosha.

(7) Avoid or make minimal use of shampoos and soaps; use oil to massage the whole body with before or after bath. This is good for dry skin as well as for general health. A massage with sesame oil is recommended.

(8) Try to stay in calm surroundings and it will be beneficial for balancing your vata if you can learn meditation.

(9) Take a lot of rest to bring down the vata. Vata is the king of doshas. If it is not alleviated, it may aggravate the pitta, which will lead to more suffering and diseases.

(10) Try to lead a regular and disciplined life to calm down the vata. Wake up on time and also exercise, work, eat, and sleep on time.

(11) Get light entertainment to relieve vata.

(12) Avoid addicting activities and substances. Addictions lead to restlessness which increases vata.

(13) Avoid dry fruits, dry mountain air, biscuits, popcorn, tea, and coffee.

(14) If you have to eat something which increases vata, you must also eat something along with it that decreases vata. This way you can always keep your dosha in balance.

(15) Vata has been compared to a finicky rabbit as it is restless and keeps running about.

(16) Vata increases in old age, so the best time to control it is when you're young.

(17) In Ayurveda, enema is used as the main therapy for vata. It does not just clear the stomach as commonly assumed, but is helpful in many other ways. Use enemas or medicines, oils or liquids (herbal concoctions, etc.) delivered through the rectum. Some recommended enemas are:

(a) Niruh (Sasneh): a concoction of medicinal liquids which helps to clear and strengthen the intestines. It should be taken on an empty stomach or three hours before any meal.

(b) Anuvasan: contains plenty of fat, hence use it only at night after eating.

(18) Always avoid:

(a) Eating curds at night and in monsoons.

(b) Drinking hot water after taking honey.

(c) Drinking milk and having anything sour.

(d) Eating hot and cold food one after the other.

(19) Unless an expert physician recommends otherwise, you can follow all the instructions listed above with great benefit.

Dietary Recommendations for People of Kapha Nature

(1) Avoid eating cold, sweet, sour, salty, oily, heavy foods. Prevention is better than cure. Avoid rice, urad dal, new wheat (can eat old wheat), sesame, olives, almonds, milk products, ice cream, sugarcane juice products, ash gourd, ridged gourd, peas, banana, guava, sweet fruits, tomato, sweet potato, coconut, dates, fresh figs (dry figs are okay), mangoes, melon, watermelon, orange, pineapple, papaya, peach, salt, paneer, and sweetmeats.

(2) Should eat pungent, bitter, dry, light, and hot foods. Spicy food is also allowed.

(3) Should eat old wheat, barley, corn, bajra, mustard, ginger, moong, masoor, gram, bathua (pot herb; a kind of spinach), bitter gourd, carrot, cucumber, garlic, onion, apple, dry fruits, honey, beetroot, cauliflower, cabbage, brinjal, green leafy vegetables, mushrooms, lady's finger, potato, black

pepper, radish, sprouts, peas, pears, pomegranate, dry fruits, etc.

(4) Exercise is important. A walk after meals is essential. Never sleep immediately after eating.

(5) Fresh foods and raw vegetables and fruits are best for kapha dosha.

(6) The spices that can be used are cumin, fenugreek, turmeric, and sesame seeds.

(7) Fast once a week.

(8) If not hungry in the morning, kapha people can do without eating breakfast or may take ginger tea in the morning instead of breakfast.

(9) Take only two meals in a day.

The constitution of every person is different. If we eat taking into consideration the vata, kapha or pitta dosha, we can avoid diseases. We need to become more aware of what we eat because every member of the family usually consumes the same food at the table, which is wrong.

Health Tips for People of Kapha Nature

Water + Earth = Kapha

Symptoms: Heaviness in the body, lethargy, tiredness, chilliness, oily skin, sweet and oily taste in the mouth, increased salivation, decreased appetite, apathy, dyspepsia, mucus in the stool, coldness in the chest, phlegm, and allergies.

Ailments: Drowsiness, constipation, itching, whiteness of skin, heaviness of the limbs, nausea, stiff joints, excessive sleep, and tiredness.

(1) Avoid fatty, salty, and oily food. Food should not be

too spicy, too sour, or too sweet. Foods with bitter and astringent tastes (present in spinach, cucumber, green vegetables) are helpful. Take dry foods. Hot food is best.

(2) Reduce sleep time. As kapha increases in the body, a person feels sleepy, but when there's more sleep, kapha increases even more, which encourages more sleep—a recipe for a vicious cycle. The kapha person should keep himself awake for most part of the day. Engaging in some interesting activity helps. They shouldn't go to sleep immediately after meals.

(3) Exercise more. Regular exercise or yoga is recommended to prevent an increase of kapha.

(4) There is imbalance of kapha in children and in cold weather, therefore be aware and learn to balance kapha when the temperature is low and special care should be taken of children's health in the cold weather.

(5) Drink water mixed with ginger and honey in the morning.

(6) Take tea with ginger or aniseed after eating.

(7) Always take a hot water bath.

(8) People of kapha nature should increase their activities instead of reducing them. Give a bit of variety to life. Sample different foods; don't always eat the same food.

(9) Don't allow diabetes to develop by eating excessive sweets.

(10) Lessen milk products and take more bitter gourd and salads.

(11) Ice cream will increase weight of people having kapha but not of those having vata.

(12) There is high tolerance to illness. This may lessen the need to consult a doctor; but due to this very fact, symptoms

of disease may appear late though the disease may have developed long back. Hence, health must not be ignored. Don't turn a blessing into a curse.

(13) Vaman or vomiting is the main therapy for kapha. Cold, cough, asthma, tuberculosis, leprosy, as well as diseases of the uterus, kidneys, and stomach, are greatly benefitted by vaman. Vaman should be done only under a physician's directions. Before vaman, it is extremely essential that complete snehpaan (intake of oils or fat) should take place. You might ask, "Is vaman just vomiting that can be easily done at home?" Not so. Vaman is more than that and involves the removal of the unnecessary fluids from the stomach and lungs with the help of medicinal liquids under a physician's guidance. This technique removes the dosha against the gravitational force, which is why it is a little troublesome, but after appropriate snehpaan, it is really not so uncomfortable. Vaman should be done early in the morning when the kapha accumulation is more. Vaman works wonderfully in children's diseases. In addition, it strengthens children's immunity and protects them from cold, cough, tonsillitis, ear diseases, nasal diseases, intense excitement, epilepsy, etc. Vaman is also beneficial for stuttering and other speech difficulties. It also boosts the intellect.

(14) There is a simple technique to freshen up the face and eyes and to wake you up. Fill your mouth with water, hold it in, wash your eyes with fresh water, and then throw out the water from your mouth.

(15) Sip a decoction of caraway. Its astringency will counteract the sweet taste in the mouth.

(16) Take hot soup and hot water.

(17) Kapha has been compared to an elephant which is heavy and walks straight.

(18) Unless an expert physician advises otherwise, you can follow the dietary and other instructions given above.

Dietary Recommendations for People of Pitta Nature

(1) The pitta patient should add more natural foods such as salads to his diet. In addition, spicy food, tea, coffee, alcohol, tobacco, and irregular eating times should be avoided as these can increase pitta.

(2) Food should be taken cold (but not stale); a little heavy food (with less oil and less salt) is permissible and eating more in the afternoon is okay.

(3) When there is an imbalance in pitta, during that time spicy, sour, salty, hot, and oily food should be avoided.

(4) Avoid urad dal, mustard, sour curds and whey, pickles, garlic, hot spices, onion, radish, tomatoes, apricot, berries, lemons, raw and sour fruits, brown rice, corn, jowar, bajra, mustard, buttermilk, meat, fish, sesame oil, almond oil, jaggery, fenugreek, asafoetida, fried foods, and hot foods.

(5) Pitta people can eat raw citrus fruits such as oranges, grapes, pomegranates, pineapples, and plums, only if they taste sweet. Also allowed are rice, barley, beetroot, white rice, jowar, meal of parched grain, lentils, fresh and sweetened curds, porridge, cow's milk, milk cream, paneer, ghee, butter, pudding, rock candy, bathua, tinda, bitter gourd, ridged gourd, coriander, mint chutney, green leafy vegetables, beetroot, lady's finger, peas, potato, sprouts, cabbage, cucumber, watermelon, green gooseberry, black raisin, banana, coconut, apple, ice cream (just a little), cherry, figs, musk melon, sultanas, green cardamom,

aniseed, saffron, turmeric, cinnamon, etc.

(6) Drink water early in the morning, an hour before lunch, and two hours after lunch. If a pitta person wants to drink water with food, it should not be more than one cup. If you drink water an hour before eating, then avoid intake of water while eating. Keep to a fixed time for meals.

(7) Take fruits and vegetables in the evenings and don't eat anything late at night.

(8) Eat sweet, bitter, cold, heavy, and fibre-rich food such as spinach, etc.

(9) Take salads with a dash of fresh lemon juice. Though sour, lemon is beneficial for pitta, and lemon juice can be taken mixed with water and a little sugar in the morning.

(10) To improve digestion and remove excessive pitta from the body, add two spoonfuls of ghee in milk and drink it two hours after dinner, once a week.

(11) Avoid being out in the sun.

(12) Take three meals in a day regularly at fixed intervals.

(13) There is more need for protein in pitta dosha, therefore include pulses in the diet.

(14) Pitta patients need a major change in diet for the alleviation of acidity symptoms which can be reduced by following one or two of the recommendations given below:

　(a) Drink cabbage juice (100 g) mixed with an equal quantity of water

　(b) Drink cucumber juice (100 g) mixed with milk (200 g) and water (400 g)

　(c) Drink one glass of coconut water with two ripe

bananas blended in milk (200 g) and water (400 g)

(d) Drink carrot juice (200 g) mixed with milk (200 g) and water (400 g)

You can use any one of the suggestions. You need to apportion fruits and vegetables (75%) and grains (25%) in your diet. Once symptoms alleviate, you can then eat fresh curds, sweet oranges, vegetable soups, watermelon, musk melon, papaya, sultanas, and raisins. After symptoms are managed, taking water mixed with honey and lemon juice in the early mornings is helpful for a deeper cure.

(14) Overeating should be avoided as this will harm the digestive system.

Health Tips for People of Pitta Nature

Fire + Water = Pitta

Symptoms: Flushed or jaundiced skin, pimples, boils, body odour, increased heat in the body, hot skin, fever, increased hunger and thirst, increased anger, heartburn, burning in the throat and stomach, heaviness of stomach after eating, sour (acidic) taste in the mouth, nausea, vomiting, loose bowels, yellowing of the stool, urine, and eyes.

Ailments: Acidity, perspiration, anxiety, redness of eyes, weakening of sense organs, non-white discoloration of the skin, a burning sensation or feeling of excessive heat in the body.

(1) Should avoid hot, sour, spicy, salty, and oily foods as well as sour curds, tomatoes, pepper, spices, and dosa (which is made of rice and eaten with spicy gravy and chutney). Cold, heavy, sweet, dry, bitter, and astringent foods are allowed.

(2) Dryness of the mouth that disturbs nighttime sleep can be remedied by drinking enough water throughout the day

and at night before sleep. Avoid watching television before bedtime and empty your mind of excessive desires and ambitions as these thoughts will increase pitta and disturb sleep. Sleep with bright and happy thoughts.

(3) Exercise regularly. Benefit from brisk walking.

(4) Avoid hot water baths; always use cold water.

(5) Keep a napkin or towel soaked in cold water over the stomach for 5-10 minutes. Once it warms, soak it again and place it around the navel.

(6) Avoid excessive stress. Avoid stressful environments for a few days until symptoms are under control.

(7) The beauty of nature can help to control your emotions. Avoid excessive stimulation and overexcitement. Self-control is the key to your health. With self-control, every disease can be controlled. With sadhana (spiritual practice) every vice of the mind can be controlled.

(8) Drink hot milk with cardamom and sugar added to it.

(9) Once a month, take castor oil or trifala powder orally at night to clear the stomach. Clearing the digestive system by consuming medicines and oils orally is called virechan. Virechan is the main therapy for pitta. In this therapy, the appropriate powder or liquid is taken orally. There are many medicines for virechan and each is beneficial if taken according to the nature of the body. Some of the medicines used in virechan are kapila, nishotar, haritaki, castor oil, jaipal, Ishabheti Vati, and other liquids. They should be taken only under doctor's advice.

(10) Pitta has been compared to a cheetah, because it is characterized by rapid digestion and speed.

(11) Pitta disorders occur more frequently during youth and in

the summer season. Therefore, one must learn to balance it before summer.

(12) Avoid fast food because they are usually overly salty or sour.

(13) Drink cold water without ice; avoid hot soups.

(14) Unless an expert physician advises you otherwise, you can follow the dietary and other instructions recommended above.

LAZINESS: THE BIGGEST SIGNPOST OF AN UNTRAINED BODY

What do you do before 9 in the morning and after 5 in the evening? Those are actually the times for you to do things outside of your usual daily routine at work or at home. Those are the times when you usually have the freedom to do what you want—free time that's typically spent resting, indulging in some entertainment, or doing some personal chores. But the fact is that your progress and self-growth actually depend on what you do during those free hours outside of your daily routine work.

It's something that most people are oblivious of, but your daily life may be wholly devoted to activities relating to family, office work, household chores, school, and other concerns that take up much of your time. Because of this preoccupation with duties, your life may get stuck in a rut and remain unchanged for a long time. It may appear to be a situation that's difficult to break out of, but the good news is that it's likely just a case of laziness.

If a change in lifestyle is what you wish, then you need to break out of your laziness and do something to allow for some change in your life which will let you move ahead. It is a fact that if you keep doing what you are doing today, you will keep getting in your life what you have got till today. Hence, you need to be aware and open up to opportunities that your laziness has kept at a distance. You must embrace life beyond your routine and see what's out there for you. The best time to do this is between 5 to 9 or your morning and evening hours. Turn things around and use these "lazy" hours to break free of your own habit of laziness.

Here are some effective steps to overcome laziness:

(1) Do some physical work every day such as yoga or gym exercise.

(2) To stop procrastinating, do one or two new tasks every day which aren't really that important and could easily be done the next day.

(3) Before going to bed at night, ask yourself if there is any other task that you could finish, and then finish it. This is an excellent way to overcome laziness.

(4) Even if you don't want to, spend some time, energy, and money to learn something new.

(5) Even if you're reluctant, try to meet new people and participate in local activities.

(6) Do some social work that may help usher in some changes in society.

(7) Join a hobby class or two that will help in developing your skills in music, dance, art, personality development, memory training, Reiki, and other useful activities.

(8) Do some writing (poetry, articles, short stories) for a newspaper, magazine, or for your own satisfaction.

(9) Once a week, write a letter or an email to people from

different fields. Develop your communication skills and learn something new about the world by corresponding with them.

(10) Self transformation can be achieved by lessening your tendency to be idle and by reducing undesirable habits like playing too much video games, excessive television, and addictions like overeating or smoking. Inaction will get you no more than the usual negative effects that you get from these bad habits. It helps to train your willpower to get rid of addictions.

(11) Every human being is unique. If you carefully observe your body, you will learn what kinds of food you should consume, in what manner, and where and when you should eat. Knowing these things will allow you to be mindful of your health.

Physical Transformation Action Plan

(1) _____
(2) _____
(3) _____
(4) _____
(5) _____
(6) _____
(7) _____
(8) _____
(9) _____
(10) _____
(11) _____
(12) _____
(13) _____
(14) _____
(15) _____
(16) _____
(17) _____
(18) _____
(19) _____
(20) _____

Part 4

Mental Transformation: Encounter with the Mind

21

THE THREE DEVILS

For mental transformation to take place, freedom from the three devils of the mind—Fear, Worry, and Anger, is essential.

Fear is a response to an external threat and usually leads to changes in our body and our actions. Generally, humans react to fear in three ways: fight, flight, or freeze. We may muster the courage to confront the source of danger (fight); we may feel terrified and try to escape (flee); or we can become immobilized (freeze). These three are the typical reactions to a fearful threat, but this book reveals a fourth way.

Worry is a general sensation of unease or distress. It is a vague feeling that causes one to be both insecure and unsure. Also expressed as apprehension, alarm, and anxiety, being worried describes an emotional state of mind expecting possible distressing events.

Anger is a feeling of seething rage which can ruin a person's life in a single moment. A person who acts in anger is impulsive in his actions and rash in his decisions. An angry individual may do the unexpected, such as abruptly resign from work or even do harm to oneself or others in a fit of rage and then wallow in regret afterwards. He may have found a fault in someone else, and hence got angry, but it's usually at his expense as the negative effects rebound on him. It follows that "anger" can be defined as "self punishment" caused by an emotional outburst resulting from an error made by someone else.

In simple words, anger is punishing yourself for others' faults. This is because anger results in pain and suffering in the individual experiencing the emotion. But at that moment the individual does not realize this. In a survey, it's been revealed that more than 80% of those in jail repent for the crimes they have committed. They've experienced firsthand how anger of even a split second can ruin a life. Anger must be tempered for transformation to occur.

THREE STEPS THAT WILL WEAKEN THE ROOTS OF FEAR

First Step: Face the Fear and There Is No Fear

Face what you fear and the fear will disappear.

If you fear going downstairs to the kitchen late at night, then make it a point to go there against your fear. The fear will disappear. Common sense says that if there is really something or someone to fear in the kitchen, it could have come to your bedroom as well. But since that's not the case, it means there is nothing to fear.

If you have a fear of your boss, what you should do is to find some pretext to go and speak to him or her about something, which doesn't have to be important. It can be as simple as a greeting in the morning or a compliment about a new tie or hairstyle. By taking the initiative, your unease will gradually fade and the result will be that you'll be less tense in the presence of your boss. This technique also works on a larger scale. If you have stage fright, then do what you can to create situations where you must speak on a stage or in a group.

It takes determined effort and courage to overcome your fear using this "face your fear" technique, but it's worth it. There was this student of Tej Gyan Foundation who had a fear of snakes. But after he understood the importance of facing his fear, he took the first step of facing his particular phobia and went to a snake park. He persuaded the officials there to allow him to have pictures taken of him while holding snakes. This helped him get over his fear of snakes and boost his self-confidence.

Second Step: Desensitize Yourself Towards Your Fear

The soles of your feet become tough, thick, and less sensitive compared to the rest of your skin because of repeated contact with the ground. The same principle of desensitization can be applied to overcome fears.

If you expose yourself often enough to the thing or situation you fear, you will eventually become desensitized to the fear associated with it, just like in the example given under the first technique—wherein you overcome the fear of going into a dark place by visiting it again and again. If, instead of a dark kitchen, you fear something else, like your boss, then you can begin to assay your fear of his authority by saying "good morning" or "good evening" to him every day. If, instead of your boss, your fear is facing people on stage, then grab every opportunity you have to go up on a stage. If the chance isn't there, then make it happen—just go on any empty stage and speak even if no one is listening or watching. With each stage appearance, your stage fear will diminish and you will gain self-confidence. It's not something that you can hurdle in one leap, but with a little willpower, you'll eventually get to the stage where you can say you're free of your fear.

Thousands of students have used this desensitizing technique successfully to overcome their stage fright. Some of them eventually reached the point where they were enjoying the stage so much that it became a problem getting them off the stage.

Whatever you fear, be it open space, water, the stage, darkness, or your boss—just face the fear repeatedly until it becomes your friend, or a thing of the past.

Third Step: Laugh at Your Fears

If you are afraid of a cockroach, you can think:

I can't believe that I am afraid of such a small creature. Ha! Ha!

As if there's reason for me to believe that it can harm me. Ha! Ha! Ha!

Laughing at your fear tends to diffuse the sensation of dread and makes you feel comfortable with the object that causes anxiety.

Consider this story. Two guys, all dressed up for a job interview, were passing a park when a bird's dropping fell on the immaculately white shirt of one of them. "Ha ha! A bird has ruined your shirt, man! Now, you're in trouble!" laughed his friend. The guy chuckled and simply scraped the dropping off with a piece of paper. "It's nothing," he said, "I am thankful that cows can't fly!" They both had a hearty laugh, and proceeded ahead.

Anyone can easily laugh in a comfy situation, but it takes courage and wisdom to laugh when there's a potentially adverse consequence. The guy who got his shirt spoiled by a bird's dropping could have given in to the fear of rejection in the interview because of a soiled shirt, but instead, he just chuckled and shrugged off the problem as if it was nothing—and indeed it was. Like the man who laughed at his friend's misfortune, we sometimes have a tendency to laugh at other people's fears and mistakes, but the better thing to do is to *not* laugh at them and instead laugh at our own fears and mistakes.

The three steps mentioned here are tantamount only to declaring war against your fear. The next three steps are part of the proclamation of your victory over fear.

THREE STEPS THAT WILL TOPPLE THE TREE OF FEAR

First Step: Apply the Law of Averages

Applying the "Law of Averages" means taking an overview of factual data related to your fear. Let us consider the following examples.

(1) A person used to fear the possibility of an accident when travelling by train. Let's see what the Law of Averages has to say about this.

- How frequently do trains run between Pune and Mumbai in a year?
    - Say about 10,000 times.
- How many accidents take place in a year?
    - 2, 3, maybe 5.
- What are the chances of an accident occurring while travelling by train?
    - 5 out of 10,000 (i.e., 0.05 percent).

In contrast to the low probability of a train accident, the chances of rain occurring when a farmer sets a schedule for tilling his field is about 50 percent for no rain, less rain, or too much rain, but he still ploughs his field. Does it make sense then, to fear something that has only a 0.05 percent possibility of occurring?

(2) A student used to fear that he would fail in his exams. What does the Law of Averages say?

- How many exams has this student taken till date?
    - Say about 100.
- Even when the student has felt a fear of failure before each of those exams, how many times has he actually failed?
    - Never. But let us suppose that he has failed once.
- So, what is the probability of his failing this time?
    - Only 0 or 1 percent.

If there is just 1 percent possibility of failing, then why be afraid? A little anxiety over an exam is actually good as it helps the student to focus. Only when the fear becomes too much should it be addressed.

(3) A woman used to have fear of lightning. How can the Law of Averages help her?

- How many people are there in her city?
    - If she lives in Calcutta, it's about 15,100,000.
- How many people get hit by lightning in this city every year?
    - About 3.
- What is the chance of her getting hit by lightning?

- It works out to something like 1/5,033,333 in a year.

Why should the woman then live in constant fear of lightning if the odds are so low?

In all these examples, 99 percent of feared incidents usually do not occur at all. Those who use the Law of Averages to free themselves of their fears gain courage, confidence, and consequently happiness.

Second Step: Rational/Logical Thinking

We all have intellect, or the capacity for rational thought, but we don't always use it. Fear in many situations can be overcome by the simple use of common sense and rational thinking.

A man was going for an interview. He was dead scared just sitting in the waiting room. In this situation, let us see how he can get over his fears with the help of Rational Thinking (RT).

Rational Thinking (RT): Are you going in there to beg for a job?

Interviewee (IW): No, I am going in there in response to their employment opportunity advertisement in a newspaper.

RT: If the interview doesn't go well, are they going to throw you out the window?

IW: No. They will not touch me.

RT: So, the worst that can happen is that you will not get the job you never even had in the first place and you will still gain the useful experience of having attended the interview.

Now that we've seen the "conversation" between the man and his Rational Thinking, what's the man afraid of if there really isn't any threat to him and he stands to lose nothing at all—in fact gaining experience in the process?

We must employ our intellect and think rationally in everyday situations that make us fearful. You can use RT to overcome most fears. If you're afraid of cockroaches, for example, you may ask the following common sense questions to yourself:

- What harm can this small creature cause me?
- Can it hurt me seriously in any way?
- Can I kill it easily if I want to?

Who should fear whom? Should I fear the cockroach or should the cockroach fear me?

RT can be applied to a number of other fears such as job insecurity. To overcome the fear of losing your job, you can tell yourself that if you do your work wholeheartedly, nothing can happen to you. At your job, apart from receiving a salary, you are also getting knowledge, experience, and skills (e.g. technical, communication, and people skills). Your boss may have the authority to dismiss you from your job, but he cannot take away all these other things from you.

Third Step: Internal Guidance—Intuition

Sometimes, you get a hunch that you'll run into someone you know. But logic tells you that it's impossible because the person isn't anywhere near you, so it's unlikely for the two of you to meet. Nevertheless, that feeling lingers on, and soon enough, your intuition proves right when that person does indeed show up or call.

In the Himalayan region, birds start to migrate towards the warmer regions just one month before snow begins to fall. These birds are never wrong and they always know when winter's coming even when the most advanced instruments fail to predict the onset of snowfall with accuracy. How do birds know when to fly away even before the threat of cold weather is even apparent? What guides these birds? The answer is intuition. We humans have the same guidance system within us.

It's a fact that we often choose one out of many options based not on factual data, but on our inner gut feeling—a choice which generally proves to be the right one, even when we think it is wrong. This is the power of intuition, and everyone, not just birds, can benefit from it.

Intuition means "tuition" or guidance from within—"in-tuition" in other words. Our intuition guides us at every moment to tell us the following, among many other things…

- What is safe for us; what is not
- Where there is danger and where it's safe
- Who is a friend; who is not

Most people fail to cultivate intuition, even though it is a real power within everyone. If you have faith in intuition, you open yourself up to receive correct guidance from it at every step of the way in life. This internal tuition, or guidance, never goes wrong. Hence, everyone must learn to listen and trust this soft voice from within. It is very important to have faith in one's intuition.

Some people who like to watch horror shows on television end up too frightened to enter a dark room afterwards, thinking that there may be someone, or something, "horrific" waiting in the shadows. In such cases it is necessary to tell yourself that if there really is any threat inside the room, your intuition will alert you about it—provided, of course, you are listening to its voice and have learned to put your trust in it.

If you're not yet aware of your intuition, then it's time to wake up and be reminded of this latent and wonderful power within you. You may have become so engrossed in your external activities (of the outer world) that you may have lost touch with your intuition (of the inner world). You can know it only through experience—by listening and observing. If you do that, you can realize that the source of guiding power is really within yourself.

Every step of yours is guided from within. You only have to develop faith and accept the fact that guidance comes from within when needed. Once you tune in to your inner guidance, your fears will dissolve, because you know that if there's any imminent threat, your intuition will warn you ahead of it.

Once in a while, do ask yourself what your aim in life is. Your intuition can help you to discover your aim. Only a few people actually work towards their aim in life with full understanding and awareness. In today's fast-paced world, there is a tendency of people to live mechanically—becoming prisoners of their daily routines and mundane rituals. To stay on track, one must therefore know and not forget his or her aim in life. If you simply go within yourself and ask what your aim is, the answer, which is crucial to you as a human being, will definitely come through your intuition.

THE FEAR LIBERATION MANTRA

The Gift of Courage

The fear liberation mantra is a gift of courage. It is the ace up one's sleeve to use against fear. Having applied the six steps described in the previous chapters, if one is still fearful, the sure way to be liberated from fear is by opening the gift of courage—which is easily done by using the fear liberation mantra:

"I AM GOD'S PROPERTY. NO EVIL CAN TOUCH ME."

This mantra is not just mere words. It is a tool of faith that is based on an understanding of the truth. This set of words has immense power and hence worthy as a mantra. If you put more emphasis on the second part, especially on the word "touch," while saying this mantra, you will see just how powerful it really is.

The mere repetition of these words will release confidence and a latent power from within. The might of these words builds a protective shield around you and the intensity with which you pronounce them determines the level of power it will generate from inside of you. The more you repeat this mantra, the stronger your mind will become to repel all the negative forces in the universe.

Why Does this Mantra Have Power?

Every word carries a certain vibration which can either improve your health or leave you prone to disease.

In ancient times, people followed the path of truth, and if anyone cursed or blessed someone, his or her words would come true. This was because words had the power of truth back then. Through the ages, words have been used more to mislead than to convey truth and hence their power waned. As a result, life in today's world is rife with hatred, jealousy, fears, tensions, lack of integrity, and weakened willpower.

Understanding the power of words is essential for them to be used for the benefit of yourself and others. To enhance the power of your words, you must do the following:

Use positive words: Instead of saying, "Don't shout," say, "Speak softly;" instead of saying, "You've failed," say, "Now you know how to win."

Use inspirational words: Use words with hope in them such as "I can," "I must," "I will," "I am fearless," "I am God's property," and so forth.

Do not be deceitful: Try not to lie. Deceit snatches power from your words, while truth enhances their power.

Don't swear: Stop using bad or abusive words.

Use words for the benefit of others: Words of prayer, blessings, hope, and growth fill the world with a new power.

Leave your house every day with positive thoughts: Recognize the power of "Happy Thoughts". Keep them in mind throughout the day.

The Power of Happy Thoughts

Negative forces get attracted only to those people who are receptive to them. These people usually approach things negatively and are scared from inside. Fearful and unhappy people tend to shrink from within and create space inside them for negative forces to occupy. On the other hand, fearless and happy people tend to expand from within keeping all the space inside filled with positive energy.

A sponge absorbs water due to its porous nature with all the holes it has. A fearful person is porous like a sponge. Don't make yourself porous like a sponge. Otherwise, you will easily absorb negative energies. Every time you feel frightened, just repeat the fear liberation mantra and all the spaces inside you will get filled, leaving no space for fear.

THE ONE HOUR WORRY CURE TECHNIQUE

A person willingly goes without food for the sake of his health or fasts out of fear of God. He can think much about the food he eats (whether he should eat something or not), the effect of what he eats on his body (whether it is healthy or not), and so on. It's important to think about the food you buy and serve because certain foods have a negative effect on the body. But such physical concern is only secondary; so what then is the primary concern?

What is of prime importance above what you eat is what your mind is fed on. Have you ever pondered on the kind of thoughts you harbour throughout the day? Are you feeding your mind with positive thoughts, or negative thoughts? These thoughts have a direct effect on you as they shape your whole life. Thoughts of worry can undermine your joy and success. It's likely that you use only two ways to combat worry—fight or flight—and you miss out on the better way, which is to face the worry. How do you do this?

The way to face your worry is to acknowledge it and recognize it for what it is without worrying over it. Face the worry methodically by allotting a fixed span of time in a day when you will not worry at all no matter what happens. This is called worry fasting. To start with a worry fast, choose an hour of the day when you will cease worrying. During that hour you should not and must not entertain any worrying thoughts at all. Don't worry, you are free to worry later as much as you want to. But for that one hour, be strict with yourself and follow through with your resolve to not worry at all whatever might happen and however terrible the events may seem. For instance, if someone tells you someone has stolen your things, say that it's not a problem and that it's your business, not his. If that person continues to bug you about the stolen things, tell him not to worry since it's not his things that were stolen anyway. Just stay calm and unfazed.

While this is just an example to emphasize the importance of not worrying during your worry fasting, it's possible in any scenario that you may be distracted by a lot of typically worrisome news and incidents that come your way. Should you encounter them, you should be prepared so as not to be affected no matter how adverse the situations.

Set aside an hour of your time in the day that suits you. The perfect time is when you are most stressed, which is usually in the morning when you are in a lot of hurry. However, some may be more anxious at work and there are those who get uptight after getting back home from the office. Instead of yielding to useless diversions like television, drinking, gambling, and gossiping, it's better to use the time to go on a worry fast. This way, you do not unnecessarily invite more worry. Instead of fleeing from worry, face it by going on a worry fast. You only need an hour. This is enough to strengthen your ability to face worry. Consider this hour as a very useful investment for a happy life.

The procedure for worry fasting is quite simple. Just make up your mind to abstain from worry for an hour and tell yourself that you will remain cool, calm, and composed for the time being. If, during that hour, something happens that may cause you to worry, just remind yourself of your commitment to complete the worry fast. You can condition your mind to worry less by practising worry fasting regularly. Once you have tasted freedom from worry even for just an hour, then the process to being completely liberated from worry would have already been set in motion.

26

DESENSITIZE YOURSELF FROM WORRY

So now that you have learned to face your worry instead of fighting or fleeing, it's now time for you to practise continuously, which serves to desensitize yourself to worry. As you've already begun to face worry by going on a worry fast for an hour a day (as explained in the previous chapter), you can now increase the time you spend not worrying about anything by going on a one hour worry fast twice a day.

Remember, you are in a war against worry. Every hour you spend in a worry fast is a battle. Win every battle and you win the war. After worry fasting for an hour twice a day, take your worry fasting up a notch by doing it for one-and-a-half hours twice a day—every day. Gradually increase the time you spend without worrying. Increase your "no worry" hours from one, to two, to three, to four, and so on, until you are able to not feeling worried at all for the whole day even in the face of adversity. The time will come when you will be completely desensitized to worry.

To be desensitized, you need to carry out the worrisome activity or get exposed to the anxiety-inducing object several times, not just once. The soles of your feet or the palms of your hands, for example are desensitized to a large extent. There was a time when your hands and feet were very sensitive, but with repeated contact with objects such as the floor, stones, and rocks for the feet; and daily activities like washing, sweeping, mopping, driving, etc. for the hands, the skin on them can become thick and tough. This same principle that makes for one's getting thick-skinned also applies to making oneself protected from worry. The effort you make to desensitize yourself against worry becomes like a game when you realize that conquering the diversion in itself is a challenge that can be quite gratifying upon succeeding and achieving your goals.

27

THREE QUESTIONS TO ANNIHILATE WORRY

Whenever you are worried, just ask yourself the following three questions. Through these questions, the truth about worry will be revealed to you.

First Question : Do events I worry about really occur?

Answer : No. Only a few of the events I worry about actually occur.

Second Question : Of the events that did occur, were they as dreadful as I had imagined them?

Answer : No. Out of the few that did occur, next to none were dreadful.

Third Question : However dreadful those events turned out, were you able to face them?

Answer : Definitely, I faced them.

Conclusion: If you have faced worrisome events in the past, won't you be able to face such events again in the future? Definitely! Then why is there a need to sit and worry over the future? Whatever you think will occur won't occur. Even if it did, it will not be as dreadful as you think it would be. And even if it were dreadful, then you can take comfort in knowing that you can breeze through such events gracefully and successfully and be able to face them again in the future. All you need to do is be honest with yourself and answer the given questions. You will realize that the habit of worrying repeatedly in your mind is a practice in futility. Through this self enquiry, a realization can be reached which eliminates worrying even in the most dreadful of situations.

Three Steps – One Formula

First Step:	Whenever you worry, ask yourself, "What is the worst that can happen?"
Explanation:	Thinking this way prepares you for the worst, whether your worst of fears come true or not. The worst that you think can happen usually does not happen at all. The chance of it happening is only 5-10 percent.
Second Step:	Accept the worst that can happen.
Explanation:	First think about the worst that could happen, then accept it. It's a fact that if you accept something that worries you, then it will no longer be a concern. Know that the failure to accept anything leads to unhappiness.
Third Step:	Take action in whatever time is left.
Explanation:	Complete the formula by taking the third step. If something undesirable will happen for a fact, then act ahead so that its effects are lessened. It's like mending a shirt that has a small tear. Since you cannot bring it back

to its original condition, the only thing you can do is mend it as best you can to prevent further damage.

This formula of imagining the worst that could happen and then accepting it before taking action to mitigate the effects is a powerful one. By applying this three-step formula, you will find that 99 percent of fearful predictions do not take place at all. Whatever you fear as the worst possible scenario has very little chance of occurring, if at all.

THE LAW OF AVERAGES WRECKS WORRY AND DESTROYS DELUSION

Parents frequently worry about their children. They have an ingrained notion that unless they worry about their children, they are not being responsible parents. It follows that if they don't worry, they are not doing their duty. What they don't know is that such negative thoughts may adversely affect their child. What parents should be doing is to be practical and apply the Law of Averages, which is not only applicable to parents who worry about their children, it's applicable to most worries.

The Law of Averages operates on a simple premise: "Worry is very much unreal since it is just a thought form. What is real is the truth." To apply the Law of Averages, ask yourself: "What does reality say? What do the facts say?" The application of this law may seem difficult, but in reality, it is the simplest and most practical. Let's try to understand the Law of Averages through this example.

Understanding the Law of Averages

Let's say a mother is constantly worried about the possibility of her child having an accident. She is plagued by these thoughts without any reasonable explanation. But it's really easy to fix the problem. All that she has to do is ask herself the facts and apply the Law of Averages:

Question : On an average, how many times has my son stepped out of the house?

Answer : Around 4000 times, assuming that the son is 15 years old and he has been going out since the age of 5 and assuming further that in 10 years he might have gone out at least once a day on average.

Question : In the past 15 years, how many times has he had an accident?

Answer : 4 times at the most.

Question : So what is the probability of his having an accident today?

Answer : It works out to 4/4000, which is only a 0.001 percent probability of getting hurt.

Question : Is there any reason that I should worry if the odds are 1:1000?

Answer : Definitely none.

This is one way you can apply the Law of Averages in dealing with worry. If you are worried about going bankrupt, then go find the average number of people who go bankrupt. It is usually a negligible amount—no more than 1 percent. If this is the case, then why worry about something that might not even happen to you?

29

LEARN TO LAUGH AT YOUR WORRIES

When things are going well, everyone can laugh and it's no big deal. But it takes courage to laugh in the face of adversity. Very few people can laugh at their problems. If you can laugh at your worries, your worries will be soothed away.

You can laugh at your worrying by looking at its futility, low probability, or your own penchant for blowing things out of proportion. Laughing at yourself, especially in situations where there is tension in relationships, lightens up the situation immediately. The ability to see the funny side of things is a good habit to develop.

Question : What will you do if someone accidentally spills a glass of water on an important document you're working on?

Answer : Let your wit do the talking. You can tell the person how fortunate you are that he doesn't drink ink.

All you need to do is see the lighter side of things and comment upon it.

Make a commitment to laugh at your worries whenever something happens that furrows your forehead from worry. Laughing at your mistakes and follies is really the best medicine for worry.

THE PROBLEM THAT IS NOT GRAVE ENOUGH TO SLAY ME CAN ONLY STRENGTHEN ME

The World is Divided into Two

Everything in life comes in pairs. For instance, there's a lesson to be learned with every problem that comes our way. If you do not learn the lesson that accompanies a problem, then the problem will only repeat itself. You'll see the logic of this rule of life in the following examples:

(1) The fear of underperforming goes hand in hand with taking an exam. Even if you somehow ace the examination, there's a lingering fear that intensifies in the next exam you take. It's not enough to study for an exam; you also need to know how to handle the fear associated with it.

(2) When someone insults you, your ego is hurt. Even if you succeed in getting the insulting person to respect you later on, but if you do not learn to manage your ego, then your problems with it continue and the next time you're insulted, you're hurt even more. Have you learnt to manage your ego?

(3) Along with free time comes boredom which can remain even if you've managed to make good of your free time by having something to do. If you have not learned to master boredom, then you will always be a slave to it and your boredom is magnified with every free time you get. Have you learned to master both your free time and your boredom?

(4) Whenever a problem occurs, stress follows. If you haven't learned to ease your stress, then you continue to be tense even after you've rid yourself of the problem. Consequently, even when you're problem-free, you tend to lead a stressful life. Have you learned to solve your problems and relieve stress at the same time?

Every Problem is an Examination

Take every problem that life throws at you as if it's an exam and the only question it has to offer is: "Are you making any progress in whatever you have learned so far?" Once you are faced with this question, then problems do not appear as problems anymore. That is why the worry liberation mantra reads as follows:

"The problem that is not grave enough to slay me can only strengthen me."

If a problem doesn't kill you, it can only make you grow with the lessons you will learn from it. Whenever a problem occurs, you will find a great change in your attitude of looking at the problem if you remember and repeat this mantra. By doing so, you will not be troubled anymore.

Anyone can say that you should learn from problems, but no one tells you how. When a problem occurs, it can appear so big that you forget to learn from it. The importance of the worry liberation mantra is that once used, it steers you towards learning something from the problem. Whenever a problem turns up, all you need to do is to ask yourself, "Will this problem kill me?" If your answer is "no," then it can only make you stronger because you learn some valuable lessons from it.

Application of the Mantra

You can apply the worry liberation mantra in more than one situation.

When your boss asks you to see him urgently in his office, the immediate thought would be that there's a problem and you feel nervous in anticipation of a reprimand or something worse. But you should ask yourself, "Is this a problem grave enough to kill me?" If "no" is the answer, then you will discover that instead of worrying, you will find the courage to go straight into your boss's office and deal with whatever is in store for you behind the door.

When guests drop in unexpectedly and you are totally unprepared to be a host to them, ask yourself the same question, "Is this a problem grave enough to kill me?" Again, if your answer is "no," then instead of becoming anxious, you will spontaneously handle the situation and learn from it. You will discover that you will have a great time with your guests.

When you are stuck in a traffic jam and you need to be somewhere in a jiffy, just ask yourself the question, "Is this a problem grave enough to kill me?" If the answer is "no," then instead of getting uptight about the situation, you will find that you are learning to manage your stress in such situations.

No matter how dire the situation—whether you're running short on money, sick, or in a quarrel, you will find yourself growing stronger by constantly applying what the worry liberation mantra has to teach. Soon, you will be able to face any problematic situation, and instead of wasting time worrying, you will be able to spend it learning and growing.

Every Problem Brings a Gift

Gold has to undergo extreme heating to be transformed into pure gold. A diamond needs to be cut and polished before it becomes a truly valuable gem. Similarly, only by facing your fears can you develop true courage. If you do not bother to do this, the incidents that trigger fear in your life will simply repeat until the lesson is learned. Remember that every problem has a lesson to teach. It is a gift that, if refused, will only cause the problem to resurface. What you should do is repeat the mantra, learn the lessons, unwrap the gifts, and say hello to a beautiful life. Once you realize the benefits of facing your fears and dealing with them, you may actually become welcoming to problems as they come.

TWELVE WAYS TO GET RID OF ANGER

Generally, when people get angry, they use harsh words, insult others, shout, scream, and even get down to hitting. If they're unable to do any of those things to the people involved, they may resort to redirecting their anger to objects around them, throwing and breaking them in frustration. Their intention is that by using any of these methods, others should agree with them and they should get what they want. If they don't get their way, they feel the need to at least express their displeasure.

Anger also means punishing oneself for others' mistakes. When you see someone making a mistake, you get angry. You may not even realize that it's self-punishment and torture brought about by anger.

Basically the cause of anger lies within us and so do its preventive measures. Let us take a look at a few measures, both short term and long term, to prevent anger.

(1) Postpone

Almost everybody is an expert at postponing things. But instead of postponing tasks, you can postpone your anger. If you feel anger arising, tell yourself that it can wait until tomorrow and then abide by your decision. If anybody has abused you or insulted you, then you must instruct yourself to postpone your angry reaction to it. The idea is to delay your response long enough to effectively extinguish the flames of anger.

(2) Think About the Consequences

Everyone spends a lot of time mulling about what they should eat or wear, but hardly anybody spends time pondering about their thinking habits and are thus ignorant of the effects of specific states of mind. For instance, do they know the consequences of entertaining certain kinds of thoughts in their head?

If you are aware of the possible effects of expressing your anger, it can be easily controlled. Cultivate the habit of asking yourself the following question whenever you are angry: "What are the negative consequences of my anger?" The answer to this question will help you douse your smouldering rage.

(3) Speak Softly

Research has proven that if you speak loudly or shout, then the propensity to anger increases. Conversely, if you speak softly, then anger is subdued. So, whenever a person is angry with you, you must make it a point to speak softly. Subdued conversation between two people expressing contradictory views will help prevent a heated argument, though it's not an easy thing to do. The natural response of people in an argument is to raise their voice. If person "A" is angry, for example, he tends to speak to person "B" in a loud voice, and as a result, B answers back in like fashion—instigating an angry exchange. That's the usual case between two individuals who don't see eye to eye. To defuse the heated situation, calm verbal discourse should be used, wherein at least one of the parties speak softly. If B responds softly to A from the start, then A will naturally reflect B's demeanour and the tendency is to calm down.

(4) Look into a Mirror

If you look into a mirror when you are angry, you will not like your own face. By looking at your facial expression which portrays your angry self, you will immediately become aware of your anger and become self-conscious enough to let the anger go. If you do not have a mirror handy, then you can use any shiny surface or just imagine looking into a mirror whenever you get angry and ask yourself the question, "Do I like the way I look like right now?" Using this technique, you will quickly become aware that your anger isn't what you need to make things any better.

(5) Drink Cool Water

Drink cool water when you get angry. It's a fact that when one is angry, the body heats up. By drinking water, the body's temperature will be reduced and this should dampen your anger at the same time.

(6) Count Some Numbers

Count from one to ten and then backwards from ten to one whenever you are angry. By counting, the focus of the mind is diverted from the anger. Counting backwards is especially helpful and works as a temporary but effective way to release anger.

(7) Utilize the Power of Words

When angry, you can repeat some affirmations or chant a mantra. You do not need to say the words aloud, but you should see to it that there is at least some movement of your speech organs. This will enable you to get rid of anger very quickly. One affirmation is: "I am cool, calm, and composed."

(8) Say the Name of God

Another technique you can use to control anger is to repeat the name of God or your guru, or if possible, visualize Him in front of you. This will inspire your spiritual side and allow your anger to dissipate.

(9) Relax

Stress is a lasting consequence of anger, and a mind that is stressed is prone to anger. If you are often tense, you can become trapped in a cycle of anger and stress. But this can be remedied by relaxation, which is similar to meditation. To know how to relax is to have the means to calm your body and mind. Relaxation meditation can be done either while sitting or lying down, although the latter is easier.

Choose the body position that works for you, and once in place, focus your attention sequentially on every part of your body—from your toes to your forehead. In whichever part you encounter stress, tell that part to loosen up and relax. The moment you give this mental command, it will relax. Move from one part to the next one. After you've gone through them all, instruct your body to completely relax and be free of stress. Such mental commands are effective in helping to relax the whole body. Your mind will also get relaxed in the process, which makes it less disposed towards anger. Where there is no stress, there is no anger.

(10) Concentrate on the Ten States of Mind and the Breath

A vital solution to anger is provided in Yoga. What yogis noticed is that the rate of breathing increases during anger. According to Yoga principles, controlling breathing makes it difficult for anger to well up to the surface. So in order to control your anger, simply take deep breaths. If you do this at the right moment, then you can successfully keep anger at bay until it dissipates.

Just as beneficial in the control of anger involves being aware of the changes in your breath whatever state of mind you are in. All that you need to do is to be mindful of the state of your mind at any given moment. This way, you can be conscious of the moment when your mind enters a negative state, and thus be able to do something about it before it gets out of hand.

Now here are ten anchors for ten states of mind. To deal with each of them, you need only become aware of the changes in your breath. Be aware of what happens to your breath when you're angry, fearful, or in any other unproductive emotional states. Note the condition of your breathing for each of the given states.

(a) **Anger:** When angry, observe the rate of your breathing—whether it is slow or fast. Also observe how your breath has lost its rhythm.

(b) **Boredom:** Boredom is like a great sickness these days. Even a child who's just three years old already has a grasp of boredom and it may come as a surprise when he or she says, "I'm bored!" The whole idea behind the distractions that society has created is for people to escape boredom by giving them the means to engage in one form of excitement or the other. Why do people jump off a cliff with nothing more than a bungee cord strapped to their ankles? What makes teenagers drag race in expensive cars? What's behind street fights? The answer to all these is boredom! But why do you have to put your life at risk when all you have to do to escape boredom is to look inwards within yourself and be conscious of what's happening to your breath at the same time? It's really that simple.

(c) **Confusion:** When you are confused, you fail to come to terms with what to do and what not to do. But if you become conscious of the state of your breath in this situation, you cause your mind to settle down, after which everything becomes clear as crystal.

(d) **Depression:** Observe the changes in your breath when you are sad, worried, or depressed.

- **(e) Ego:** Your ego may get bruised as a result of a hurtful incident, and this triggers a series of arguments within yourself. To ease out of this internal conflict and quiet your internal chatter, pay attention to what is happening to your breathing.

- **(f) Fear:** Every person is afraid of one thing or another in life. Fear, be it small or big, does in fact affect one's breathing. But if you gather enough patience to focus on your breath when feeling scared, you open the way to control the fear.

- **(g) Greed:** Greed brings about a subtle change in breathing. If you are conscious of your breath when you feel greedy or yearn for something in excess of what you really need, then you can detect this change and allow yourself to hold the reign on your primal impulses. It's pretty useful when, after winning a sum of money in a game of chance, you may feel the need to win much more—which can lead to you losing what you've already won.

- **(h) Hatred:** Switch to being aware of your breath when thoughts of hatred for someone start to make their presence known inside your head.

- **(i) Ill will:** If the intent to harm somebody arises within you, just concentrate on your breath to get rid of it. This way, ill will does not gain power over you.

- **(j) Jealousy:** When you're jealous, your breathing loses its rhythm and this should alert you that this emotion is out to take control of your mind and body.

(11) Strengthen Your Willpower

A person who does not have willpower also lacks self-confidence. Without self-confidence, a person does not really get rid of fear and anger and retains the tendency to be overcome by these emotions even in situations that do not merit them. This person will also be immobilized at times by the fear of failure and may get frustrated or disappointed with everything unexpected that happens. Due to this fear, the feelings of irritation and anger arise, even due to things of little consequence. It's easy to get caught up in a vicious cycle and the only way to come out of it is to strengthen one's willpower.

Every person makes promises to himself and to others, but if he is unable to fulfil them, his willpower begins to diminish. It follows that one should not make a promise that cannot be kept. If you have made a vow, you must fulfil it. If you're not used to this, it can help to practise with minor promises, such as committing to study for two hours straight or opting to go without lunch on this particular day. These little promises do not have to be significant in the least, but they can help to strengthen your willpower. As you fulfil small promises like these, you can take up bigger ones as you go along. Little by little, you add to your self-confidence.

Try performing this experiment (mentioned earlier in the book) before you go to sleep. Just before you hit the sack, ask yourself, "Is there anything else that I can do before I go to sleep?" If you find out there really is something else you can do, then go ahead and get it done even if it's trivial and not even urgent. By pushing yourself to complete one such task every night, you make your willpower stronger. Practise consistently, and you can hone your willpower and eventually be free from debilitating anger and fear.

(12) Getting Angry Is A Choice

It doesn't help to get angry in the usual way every time. Have you noticed that when people get angry, they do things like scream and throw objects around in the same manner every time? These actions are what we usually associate with anger and they're not really pleasant; additionally they do not yield any positive result. Now here is a technique wherein you can allow yourself to get angry when necessary but end up doing things differently. The trick is to condition yourself to adopt a different demeanour every time you get angry. By being creative in how you express anger, you can influence people around you to a great extent. Write down a few ways of expressing anger and pick one of them to "use" when the situation allows it. It should be no different from how we choose one thing over another in life. For our purposes, you will choose an acceptable manner in which to express anger.

Let us consider a story to understand this point. A teacher used to tell young school children that their appearance should always be neat—with shoes polished, shirts pressed, etc. But the problem was his students hardly practised what he taught. One day, in frustration, he allowed himself to express his anger—but in a unique and non-confrontational way. He got a brush and shoe-polish, then sat outside the classroom door and announced, "I am going to polish the shoes of students whose shoes aren't clean." The students didn't know how to react. They were flabbergasted and felt ashamed. They learned their lesson and promised never to wear unpolished shoes again to class.

It's not easy to express anger creatively. It takes courage for this approach to be taken. While there are times when you cannot help but express your anger, however, let it always be your choice, and not something that arises out of impulse without your being aware of losing your composure and regretting your outburst later on.

MIND POWER AND CONCENTRATION MEDITATIONS

Practise the following meditations and exercises to improve your mind power and encourage mental transformation at the same time.

Tuning Meditation

For the tuning meditation, it is essential to know how to concentrate in order to go inwards within ourselves. This meditation is useful for tuning the mind, intellect, and Self.

(1) Close your eyes and sit in an appropriate meditation posture with a suitable mudra. Mudra is a symbolic hand gesture or an appropriate manner of positioning palms and fingers.

(2) Close your eyes and visualize two single-digit numbers. Multiply the numbers among themselves and remember the answer.

(3) Next, visualize a pair of two-digit numbers, like 47 x 22, then multiply them by each other.

(4) While multiplying, don't use any mathematical or memory technique. Do the multiplication in your mind as you would do math on paper.

(5) When you get the answer, open your eyes. Do the same computation on a piece of paper to check the answer. In this problem, the number 22 was used, which is made of two of the same digit (i.e. 2 and 2). So, what did you feel while doing this exercise? Did the numbers stay firm in your mind for some time and then begin to slip away? With this type of mental exercise, you can enhance your concentration and mental power, which are both useful in beginning meditation. And were you conscious of any thoughts? During that time, all your other thoughts had disappeared! This is exactly the importance of this exercise—you become conscious only of the here and now. You learn to live in the present; otherwise thoughts are constantly taking you either in the past or in the future. Additionally, you will also learn how to rest and relax the mind with meditation—relieving it of the stress of running about back and forth. Thus, if you have thoroughly learned the art of meditation, then you will have also mastered the secret of keeping your mind uncluttered by thought and therefore always feeling fresh.

(6) If you had problems in the second experiment, then you can do another one that's pretty much similar but easier. How much is 47 × 47? Close your eyes and calculate. Since you're using the same two-digit number twice, there is less possibility of you forgetting or miscalculating them.

(7) Now try to mentally calculate the answer for 47 × 29. Understand that getting the correct answer is not what's important. The objective of this experiment is to improve

mental alertness. Initially you could multiply double-digit numbers, with one number made up of two identical digits. After doing that you'll see how easy it is to mentally multiply double-digit numbers, both of which have different digits.

(8) Those of you who are able to do this multiplication exercise easily should move on to three-digit numbers. If that's too difficult, you should begin with single-digit numbers. When you are able to accomplish these multiplication exercises easily, you can move on to higher digit numbers.

Sound Meditation

(1) Close your eyes and sit in the meditation posture with a suitable mudra.

(2) Keeping the body steady, listen to all the sounds around you. Try to hear and identify five different sounds.

(3) If you clearly hear the sound of an electric fan, for instance, then you must hear beyond that to detect various other audible sounds contained in that sound. You should listen for these secondary sounds carefully. The other ambient sounds audible could include conversations of people, children laughing and playing, the clattering of dishes, or the clacking of a computer keyboard. There could be jarring sounds like the blaring of a truck's horn or the slamming of a door, but there could also be soft sounds like the sound of feet walking on carpet or the hum of a refrigerator. Other artificial sounds could be those of the television, radio, CD player, and vehicle engines. On the other hand, there could be the pattering of rain, the thunder, or the whoosh of the wind. These sounds are common almost everywhere. But if, for some reason, you

are in a room with hardly any perceptible sound, like your bedroom, then try to perceive the sound of silence. Feel the stillness.

(4) Try to detect every type of sound around you. If you live near an airport, for example, you will often hear the sound of airplanes, and if you listen carefully, you will notice that all airplanes don't sound the same—every airplane has a different sound. Try to identify even the minutest of sounds in the din of louder sounds. You can do this with your eyes closed, and you'd be surprised at how many different sounds you can hear this way. Once you've identified at least five different sounds, open your eyes.

(5) Practise the sound meditation exercise every day. With each passing week, you can go on increasing the number of sounds you can detect.

Breathing Meditation

(1) Sit in a proper posture with a proper mudra for meditation.

(2) Relax yourself by taking one or two deep breaths and then releasing the air slowly.

(3) As you begin the meditation, let your breathing continue as it was before—whether shallow or deep, fast or slow. Allow it to continue comfortably and naturally… don't try to control your breathing. If you try to control it, then it is not meditation, it is breath regulation or pranayam.

(4) Be aware of the breath going in and coming out. Feel how it goes in and how it comes out. Observe from which nostril the breath is moving in and out—the right, the left, or through both nostrils. Be aware of the direction of your breathing and whether your breath is warm or cold.

(5) Concentrate the mind on the inhalation and exhalation

of your breath. Be aware of the air going in as you inhale and acknowledge the breath coming out as you exhale. In it goes, out it goes. Just be conscious of your breathing.

(6) While keeping the body steady, continue to be aware of your every breath as your lungs draw in and release air. Sometimes your breathing will be deep; sometimes shallow.

(7) Practise this breathing for 20-45 minutes as you find convenient. After some days of practice, when you become used to this meditation, then you can meditate on the interval between two breaths.

Interval Meditation (Feel in the Blank)

(1) Begin this meditation in the same way as you did with the Breathing Meditation. Maintain awareness of your breath moving in and out of the nostrils.

(2) There is an interval between when the breath goes in and when it comes out. The interval always exists, even if for only a millisecond. Concentrate on this gap when the breath is neither going in nor coming out. (Feel the blank instead of filling it.) A similar interval exists in between two thoughts. We tend to fill this interval with more thoughts, which is the reason why there's always chatter inside our head. Meditation clears the mind of this mental chatter and connects us to the heart—not the physical heart, but the one that's our spiritual centre.

(3) After exhalation of one breath and before the next breath is inhaled, there exists a moment in time when there is no breathing activity. Notice that moment and be aware of it as your breath cycles. Your breathing should continue normally and you don't have to worry if you miss a gap. To become aware of that moment of non-breath, simply

pay attention to the next breath you'll be taking.

(4) The interval meditation can be done anywhere and anytime since we are always breathing.

Thought Meditation

(1) Close your eyes and sit in the meditation posture with a proper mudra.

(2) Start watching your thoughts. See what thoughts are going on inside you.

(3) Keep your body steady and continue viewing the different thoughts in your mind as if from a distance (without identifying yourself with them and remaining detached). Through this separation, you will know what kind of thoughts go through your mind and the kind of subject matter they contain.

(4) Continue watching your thoughts as if you're a witness. Don't label any thought as good or bad. Avoid any desire such as: "I don't want any thoughts" or "I want more thoughts." Such conscious patterns should be avoided in order to keep the natural flow of thought.

(5) Initially practise this meditation for 5 minutes and then gradually increase the time. When you become used to it, then you can begin with the thought numbering meditation.

Thought Numbering Meditation

(1) This meditation is meant to bring about thoughtlessness; where thoughts are eliminated from the mind by numbering them in sequence. Begin the meditation by watching every thought.

(2) Start counting every thought. As soon as a thought arises,

count it in your mind. The first one is number one; the second, number two, and so on. Continue counting thoughts in this manner as you go deeper into the meditation.

(3) Sit quietly even if there appears to be no apparent thought; or if the thought about not having any thought arises such as, "I don't think I'm thinking of anything right now," then count this as well, as it's also a thought.

(4) Don't dwell on any thought. Just count it and let it pass.

(5) With this meditation, you can significantly reduce the number of your thoughts. Sometimes you may reach a thoughtless state. This meditation should be practised regularly but without expecting any specific results. You will see that it will work in its own time.

Eagle Meditation

The eagle is a bird that sees things clearly from above. Its vision is amazingly sharp. In the same way, meditation can be done with the eyes open, capitalizing on our sense of sight to see things more clearly just like an eagle. Therefore this type of meditation is known as Eagle Meditation.

(1) With eyes open, try to notice all the red objects around you. Once you wake up in the morning, notice all the red objects as you get up from the bed to go to the bathroom. See if you can find at least five red objects.

(3) The colour to find doesn't always have to be red. Make a resolution every day to notice objects of a specific colour. You can look for green objects on one day; blue on the next day; orange on the third day; and so forth. Since we only know a limited number of colours, it makes sense to consider shades of colours such as light blue, dark blue,

and others, when performing the Eagle Meditation. You may discover that some colours are harder to find than others, but if they're there, you'll find them. You only have to look more carefully.

(4) Through the Eagle meditation, you develop the ability to notice objects in your home like an eagle spots its prey from a distance. Our lack of attention to detail has made us unaware of the things present in our usual surroundings, like in our home. But with this meditation, you improve your ability to observe. Using it, you will discover that there are places where you hardly look at or even notice at all. You have effectively stopped seeing such places and things. But this meditation will allow you to start seeing again and to be truly conscious and aware of what your eyes see.

"I Don't Know" Meditation

(1) In the "I don't know" meditation, all known labels to objects have to be kept aside.

(2) When you look at any object, like a wall clock in your house, tell yourself, "I don't know what this thing is." Whenever you see anything or anyone in your house, don't "see" it as something familiar. If you see your mother, you should think, "I don't know this person," then look at her face carefully. You may be surprised to find so many changes in your mother's face, which you hadn't even noticed before. This is because you had lost your ability to really see what you're looking at. Your labelling her as "Mom" makes you less predisposed to seeing her as you would see someone else because you may feel, 'It's mom; what's there to be seen?' In other words, true seeing has ceased and it shouldn't be that way. Thus, if you look at something

familiar, like a chair, don't think that it's a chair. You have to look at it as if you're seeing it for the first time and ask yourself what it is.

(3) After having seen every object in a room without the benefit of labelling through familiarity, your surroundings will come alive with colour and detail. Every object will feel more alive and you will not have to deal with boredom anymore. Seeing in this manner changes your perspective. This is how you learn to "see" again in the "I don't know" meditation.

Gratitude Meditation

(1) Close your eyes for 2-3 minutes.

(2) Look at yourself through your mind's eye. Imagine your duplicate or clone who is exactly like you, but blind.

(3) Look at the entire life of your blind clone. How is it leading its life from morning to night? Look at what difficulties it faces due to blindness. Imagine how your clone would live your daily life.

(4) While imagining all this, feel all your clone's suffering arising from those difficulties.

(5) Then make your clone disappear. Now you should realize how lucky you are to have the gift of sight and you will be filled with gratitude because you don't have to face all the difficulties of the blind. Thank the heavens for this.

(6) On the second day of this meditation, imagine your clone to be deaf and imagine all of its difficulties. Allow yourself to be filled with gratitude since you are not deaf and thank God for the gift of hearing. The feeling of gratitude makes you sensitive and receptive. It allows you to understand more of the pain and suffering of others.

(7) In like manner, take up a blessing each day and imagine how your life would be without it by visualizing your clone. This will enable you to feel the grace that you've received but ignored. Remember that without contemplation, even diamonds are mere pieces of coal.

Part 5

Financial Transformation: Encounter with the Intellect

MISCONCEPTIONS ABOUT MONEY

For transformation at the financial level, it is important to understand misconceptions and myths about money.

Three Misconceptions Related to Money

(1) Money Is Everything, Money Is God

Some people believe that money is everything. Hence, they want to hoard it or hide it. For such people, money is God. They do not have any space in their lives for love and relationships.

Transformation at the financial level does not mean that you spend lavishly or that you hoard money. It means that you must understand the idea of money correctly so that you nourish the right thoughts to attract it and ultimately attain it with ease.

(2) Money Does Not Mean Anything

Some people give no value to money and spend recklessly whatever they earn. These people may not give any deep thought to money as a resource to be managed. But beyond spending, money does have its significance. The beauty of money is that it enhances whatever it touches. Money is the catalyst that allows your internal world to engage with the external world.

(3) One Should Run Away from Money

Some people perceive money as something that will corrupt them and therefore they always keep running away from it. They consider it to be an evil aspect of the material world and even the mere touch of money can make them feel scandalous. But more money does not mean less spirituality or fewer relationships. More money simply means—more money. It's a means to financial freedom to enable you to go through the process of transformation more easily. Money is a tool towards an easier life but not the goal itself.

So now that you have seen how people differ in their perception of money and the manner they use it—some spend it recklessly; some hoard it; and still some run away from it—ask yourself the following questions:

(1) How can money be God?

(2) How can money be filth?

(3) How can money be like a serpent that has to be avoided?

The fact is that money is nothing but money. Once you learn to be comfortable with money, you would have already taken the first step towards financial transformation.

Thirteen Myths about Money

You will never achieve financial transformation unless you resolve conflicting beliefs about money which are often instilled by your parents.

Many children are indoctrinated by their family to believe that it is "wrong" to borrow or owe money, among other things. Many are taught that businessmen are all dishonest or unethical. Others are led to believe that big financial dreams are nothing but foolishness.

With all these ingrained beliefs, they develop poor money values that becoming rich is not possible for them.

To get rid of negative beliefs or thoughts on money—also known as money myths—you must identify them first. Here is a list of money myths, blocks, and "negative money messages" that may reflect the way you view money:

(1) It is difficult to earn money.

(2) People do not repay the loans they take from others.

(3) Money is filthy. Money is bad.

(4) More money means more complications and difficulties.

(5) Money is the Devil / Money is God.

(6) Money does come to me, but seems to easily slip away.

(7) I should not lend money on auspicious occasions.

(8) Money makes enemies of friends.

(9) The rich are bad.

(10) Money will come to me now since my palms have begun to itch.

(11) There is less money, less happiness, and less time in life.

(12) More money means less spirituality.

(13) I can buy anything with money.

These are only some of the myths about money. What's interesting is that even if these are merely myths, but if you believe in them, they will be made manifest in your life. Then you will see the power of the beliefs you adhere to.

Two Approaches to Money

There are two approaches to money: Poverty Approach and Prosperity Approach. The Poverty Approach means you always think that you lack money. In other words, you are always looking at others' money and feeling bad because you think they are better off than you are. You feel hopeless and helpless when it comes to money. If you think you are poor, you are. Thinking that you lack something in any way is a mindset that cuts you off from your real power. It is deficiency thinking, wherein you think you need more money, when you're only trying to get something to fill the deficiency you feel inside. Thoughts of deficiency always backfire. They attract circumstances that drain you of what you already have. On top of that, even if you get all that you think you need, it doesn't change your mindset. Deficiency thinking always makes you yearn and strive for more instead of recognizing and appreciating what you already have. Applied to your finances, all that is upgraded is the amount of money you want, and not what you actually have. So, no matter what the situation is, you continue to suffer over not having enough money.

Prosperity Approach to money is the opposite of Poverty Approach. People who are prosperous do not feel deficient, and therefore, they do not look at what they don't have and instead focus on what they do have. They say things like, "I have all that I need to be happy. I am happy and completely satisfied." It isn't that they are lazy or complacent; they just recognize and appreciate what they have. They also know that in the midst of their circumstances, tomorrow will always bring something new, and the fruits of their labour will eventually ripen for the picking. This is because they understand that everything is always changing anyway, and hence if they want to, they can be happy and satisfied tomorrow as well, no matter what. Prosperous people know that nothing is constant and that they can always grow with change. They do not believe that circumstances in their life determine their happiness. They know that events do not define their life—it's how they react to them that matters.

With this kind of Prosperity Approach thinking, anything is possible.

It lets you experience the abundance of the present and of the future right now. It opens you to knowing that prosperity does not come from having things turn out the way you want them to. Prosperity comes from knowing that you can find peace and happiness no matter what happens. Prosperity is not something external for you to pursue. It is something inside of you. In fact it is you.

If you harbour thoughts that you are somehow unworthy of prosperity, then what you are essentially saying is that others deserve prosperity but not you. These thoughts of unworthiness tend to grow if you hold on to your unfounded belief of unworthiness. The fact is that you are every bit as deserving of abundance as any other person. To experience abundance, you must accept yourself as completely worthy and as deserving as any other person. It's not a requirement that you be perfect or special. No one is perfect but everyone is certainly special. All you need to know is that you are worthy. The simple fact that you are alive is already proof of your worthiness.

The mindset for prosperity is that of fulfilment and contentment, without jealousy. When your life is filled with contentment and fulfilment, you will be able to give some of these to others and this action will allow you to receive the same in return. It's the way of nature. So, be happy for the abundance of others and send them love and joy. All that you give will come back to you a thousand-fold. But you must remember that if you are really serious about being prosperous, you should know the importance of doing everything with love and not to be overly concerned about the rewards or money that might come your way. A prosperous heart is filled with the faith that all things will work out well. A prosperous heart serves others without too much concern about the money to be made.

Prosperous people do not put their money or their self-interest first. They do what they do because they love what they are doing and they are happy to be of service. They are driven by an inner desire to make a contribution to the world. As a result, rewards fall into their laps like how ripe fruits drop off the trees of an orchard when the right time arrives. Fulfilment, in every area of your life, comes from giving, not getting. Giving is always the key to abundance. The single-most important mindset for manifesting prosperity is to shift your thinking from getting to giving.

Real power does not come from anything outside of us—least of all from having money. If that were true, then we would be powerless without it. Real power comes from within. It comes from becoming a better person. It comes from giving, sharing, and connecting with the ultimate purpose of your life (See Part 7). Money and objects associated with prosperity come naturally into your life as a result of this. In fact, money is just one of the many things that come to you for living a life of gratitude, giving, and sharing.

THE SECRET OF FINANCIAL GROWTH

What you give is beneficial because you progress through giving. What you take merely provides sustenance, but giving makes you grow and develop into a better person. Additionally, according to the law of nature, whatever you give will come back to you in one form or another, multiplied many times.

This is a great secret that applies not only to money, but also to time, love, attention, and so many other important things in life. Hence, you must learn to give. You get a lot of opportunities to give, as something is always being sought from you by others. Giving to others is well and good, however, you have to give something to yourself too. Generosity is not only for others; it's for you as well. While most people are able to give to others, they are unable to give anything to themselves. You can do this by dividing your resources into ten parts. You can divide your time into ten parts, give yourself one part and distribute the remaining nine parts between the house, the office, and for service to others. It's good to be generous, but it's essential that you give one part of your time to yourself.

Similarly, divide whatever money you earn into ten portions. You will spend nine of the portions to pay for basic services like water, electricity, the laundry, groceries, other expenses, and even give to charity. The remaining one part of your wealth must be given to yourself. If you do this, you will begin to understand the secret of giving. There's a saying that whatever you give makes you develop and grow. This can be vague to many people, so let us try to understand this through the following illustration.

A man has seven days to finish a piece of work. Given the seven days of work time, the job gets completed only on the seventh day. However, if the man had only two days to do the work, he would have finished it in just two days. Since the man had seven days, he consumed all the time given to him. People tend to spend what they earn in a similar manner, wherein entire earnings are disposed of to meet basic needs. The secret of financial growth suggests that if you earn something like ten thousand rupees, you must set aside one thousand and live off the remaining nine thousand. If you stick to the notion that your income should be in excess of what you earn at present in order to vanquish your money problems, then your wish will not be realized because your next thought will always be about the necessity of earning even more to meet your needs.

The amount of money you earn is really inconsequential. The person who earns three hundred rupees may think the same way as someone who earns three thousand, or someone who earns thirty thousand. If they all believe that their financial problems will cease only if they can get more money, then they simply do not understand the secret of giving a portion of your wealth to yourself and treating that portion as your personal treasure. The denomination and currency also do not matter. Thus, even if it is ten rupees, a hundred pesos, or a thousand yen—the principle is the same, and that is to treasure that which you have given to yourself while spending the rest for living expenses. This kind of budgeting will suffice so that all of your needs are met if you spend wisely. Never think that it won't happen, because once you do, you lose the crucial belief which will allow you to meet your goal of prosperity.

Invest Your Savings

Let us see what you can do with the one portion that you have saved for yourself. With the help of a good financial advisor, you can invest it in a productive way so that your money multiplies. Lots of people make the mistake of eating up their savings as it grows. Let's study this a bit more.

Supposing you have money in the bank and you get interest on it. Now let's say you want to spend that extra money to party or you want to buy things that will only make you look wealthy even when you're not. If this is what you want, then it is likely you don't know the "secret" to financial growth yet—that this money, if reinvested, will bring good returns. With understanding and intelligence, even the small amount of your savings can prove to be the seed that can grow into a big tree full of money. You can thus enjoy your present in peace. The alternative to this is to be weighed down with financial worries all your life.

Make the Budget Your First Advisor

After saving and investing one portion, make a reasonable budget plan for your needs with the nine portions left of your money. You must write down all your expenses. All these will have to be adjusted within the limits of the nine portions. Let the budget serve as your first advisor or your finance minister. Heed what it says and soon you will get to know what items it is suggesting to you and what it is telling you to avoid. At the start, you may find this difficult, but later you will be surprised at how everything falls into place, and how all your needs are being met at the same time that your money grows. In this way any concern about insufficient wealth or not having enough money gets resolved.

Make a Magic Box

Having fulfilled all your needs within the nine portions, if you have a list of some special desires that can't be adjusted within the available budget, create a special "magic box" for it. Write those wishes on a piece of paper and put it in that box. Tell yourself that these wishes will be fulfilled through miracles. Write "I expect miracles daily" on that box and say to yourself, "I leave this box to God to fulfil my wishes. I will spend only on those items that have been accounted for in my budget."

Don't Get Lured by Schemes

No matter how much you think you are smart enough, there's always a chance that you may get conned. Hence, do not be taken in by tempting, seemingly innocent schemes. Con men will advise you that you can easily multiply your money several-fold by investing with them. Beware of these fake agents. Go for the valid businesses that you've verified. Don't trust your luck with lotteries only to feel sorry later on. Some people may get lucky betting on the lottery but the fact is that Lady Luck doesn't favour anyone in a consistent manner. Some may make easy money over a short time, but in the long run 99 percent of people ruin their savings in lotteries.

One likely outcome, when you suddenly make easy money, is that you squander it on foolish and useless things. The money is gone and all that you are left with are some unfulfilled desires. Can you imagine a situation where the cravings keep popping up, because you got used to them while you had the cash, but now there is no money left to satisfy those cravings?

Another possible outcome after making easy money is when the person gets too concerned about keeping the money safe. In the process he makes his family unhappy and he himself becomes miserable. Why? Because he has assumed that now he has the power over the money when in fact it's the other way around—it's the money that has power over him. He knows he does not have the capability to make that kind of money, so he keeps it to himself for fear of losing it. Hence just having some money at present is not what's important—it's your capacity to earn that is.

Increase Your Capacity

Every individual's earning capacity is based on his qualities, skills, and capability. Therefore, strengthen your qualities, develop computer skills, learn new languages, work sincerely, and provide good service. All these things will make a more "bankable" person out of you and consequently the inflow of money in your life will increase. Recognize opportunities; good luck always follows them. Capabilities and opportunities are what will bring in more money to you.

Be Responsible and Careful with Money

Those who make a decision about money at the right time reap the benefits of that decision. There is a saying about how the Hindu Goddess of Wealth, Lakshmi, is pleased with those who prove capable of looking after their money. If you have not been able to prove that, then how can the Goddess be pleased with you? Observe Goddess Lakshmi pursues which kind of people and whom she eludes. She avoids irresponsible people but surrenders to those who are careful, wise, and those who free themselves from an uncertain future by fulfilling their future goals today through good financial planning. If you note the money mistakes you are currently making and strive to learn from them, your future shall be bright. Actions need to be carried out wisely in the present for them to have the desired effect in the future.

You must prove to yourself that you can take care of your money and use it wisely, such that even the small amounts that you earn on investments are also kept safe. How will you demonstrate your eligibility for prosperity if even the small amount that you save is not safe from yourself? Even if you give money to charity apart from what you allot for all your expenses, the total of that amount must come out of the 90 percent of your income. The part that is retained for yourself should be 10 percent. It may be small, but you must regard is as a treasure to be grown like a seed that can turn into a big tree.

So it pays to make a habit out of keeping one part of your regular income for yourself, though this is easier said than done. Small amounts of money earned work like a switch for some people who get the urge to spend impulsively on things—a signature jacket, a pair of branded sandals, a treat to colleagues. But what does this prove? While this makes you look rich, it doesn't make you rich, because you lose money in the process. The only thing it proves is that you are unable to hold on to your money. If you are short on money or unable to attract more of it, then it raises a question on your capability as regards money. So ask yourself, "Have I become capable enough to make money, save it, and make it grow?"

Escaping the Clutch of Postponement

Procrastination, or the habit of postponing things for another time, is an expedient you don't really need. You have to come out of the clutches of postponement, wherein you keep making promises to yourself to start saving or investing but never really getting to the matter. Tomorrow turns into yet another tomorrow; for instance, you plan to make a deposit in the bank and you procrastinate. You then end up not depositing the money and spend it on something you don't really need. You have to do away with this habit because it makes you lose money and time. Losing time is also losing money in case of saving and investments since you lose out on the interest or dividends.

Pay Back Your Debts

Debts need to be paid back because they block your progress to wealth. As long as there is a block, the money will cease to flow in. However, if you are not in a position to pay back at present, go to your creditors and tell them that you will start saving a portion of your earnings to pay them back. Appeal to them for their support and to give you the time you need. Assuring them this way will make your lenders feel better that the money they lent you is guaranteed to return. Until you do this, they will likely be under the impression that you might not pay them back. But with your clear plan for payment presented, they will have a reason to help you and give you both the time and the strength to be freed from the debt.

In this chapter you have learned a very important secret of life and how it relates to money. With the lessons learned, your way to prosperity is now paved and easier to travel on. In the next chapter you will learn about the twelve prosperity secrets.

TWELVE PROSPERITY SECRETS

(1) Instil the Habit of Saving

There is a little story that teaches the vital habit of saving. A long time ago, there was this young boy who used to buy peanuts daily from a vendor for one rupee. He always used to complain about how he never had enough money, due to which he had to live only on peanuts most of the time. One fine day, months after the boy first bought peanuts, the vendor gave the boy a huge bag full of peanuts. The boy refused to take it saying he cannot accept charity and can neither pay for it. The vendor shook his head and smiled. "This bag of peanuts is yours! I used to save two or three nuts from your purchase every day. With time, there were enough nuts saved to fill this large a bag." The incident was an eye-opener for the boy. After that, he stopped complaining and began saving every day.

No matter what your income is, an amount of regular savings, no matter how small, can eventually surprise you with the amount that gets accumulated in time. Everything accumulates over time, and savings are no exception. But to make it work, you may have to put in a lot of tiny bits of money and effort that nobody might even care to know about. It's like an avalanche which starts out as a small, dislodged pebble, but then grows as tons of dirt, small stones, and snow are set loose to become a mass of debris that goes down the mountain slope with increasing force, levelling everything in its path.

Every large fortune is like an avalanche which started out small. It's simply the result of an accumulation of hundreds or thousands of small change. To start growing your own fortune, you only need to set aside a small amount of money regularly and watch it grow into a fortune. You can start saving right now, setting the motion for your money to accumulate. By doing so, you will also begin to attract all the money that you ever need in your life.

(2) Make Money Your Need, Not Your Want

One of the major causes of human problems is the tendency of comparison. Most individuals think, "If my neighbour has purchased a car, then I must buy one too."

However, before buying anything, you must ask yourself, "Do I really need it?"

When your purchase is a "need," it simply means that the item bought is an essential or a necessity, because you can't imagine life without it. Food and clothing, for example, are necessities. It also includes objects which are very useful and can be used daily.

On the other hand, your purchase is a "want" when the item is something that you simply like and only wish to have only because you see others owning it. Basically, it's just something that's nice to have, but isn't necessary for your survival or basic comfort. An example of a "want" could be a very expensive branded watch or the latest cell phone when you already have a good one.

Whenever you feel like buying anything, ask yourself the question: "Need or Want?" Take a deep breath and think. If the answer is

Want, answer a few more questions: Are all your needs fulfilled? Do you have the necessities for your household, such as groceries or medicines? Are your children or other family members provided for? When you answer these questions, keep in mind that you can definitely spend on Wants, but only after all your Needs have been fulfilled. More than half of your money problems will be solved with this Need or Want method.

(3) Money Should Always Flow

Some people hide their money instead of using it or donating it. They never bring their money out in the open. It's the wrong thing to do, because after a time, money will stop flowing into their lives, whether they like it or not.

Money is akin to energy. You could say it is like a flowing river, strong and seemingly never-ending. But when a flowing river gets blocked, it stagnates and gets silted by dirt and sewage. Eventually it dies out.

Making money flow doesn't mean that you have to spend it lavishly. It only means you should spend it with an intention that it will multiply and come back to you. There is a law of nature according to which whatever is given will come back many times over. This law applies not just to natural elements like air and water, which are cycled in the environment. It's just the way of everything, including money.

Consider the following give-and-take cycles in everyday life:

(1) Say soothing words and you get them back.

(2) Give love and you receive love.

(3) Give a helping hand and you'll be lent a hand when you need it.

(4) Pray for someone and you get the fruits of prayer.

(5) Say bad words and you get bad words in return.

The principle works like a boomerang, which, when you throw, comes back to you. It's also like the echo of your voice that rebounds on a rock face. This is nature's principle and it is working all the time. It does not matter whether you believe it or not. Nature does not work based on any individual's beliefs. It has its own method of working and we're subject to it.

A society or a country will never prosper if there is no flow of money. But those who know the nature of money easily make more of it by letting it flow naturally, thereby completing the kind of cycle that nature smiles upon.

(4) Avoid Blockages that Hamper Money Flow

The biggest blockage to money flow is the worrying we do about money. When thinking about money becomes worrying about money, the flow of money, which is vital for more money to come in, gets clogged. When you entertain negative thoughts about money, it's like you're introducing a clot into the bloodstream. It may even lead to the equivalent of a heart attack. Blood must always flow for it to give life to your body; likewise, money must always flow to be of any use in your life and to be able to grow. Often, the blockages to money flow lies with individuals, such as the miser, who is akin to a clot in the bloodstream. Penny pinching blocks the liquidity of money not only in the life of an individual, but also in a country, or even society as a whole. A single person can sow the seeds of many money blocks in a lifetime. Whenever you cheat, hoard, or take what's not yours for the sake of getting rich, you are setting up a money block and telling your subconscious mind and nature itself that "I do not deserve money legitimately."

Here are some examples to illustrate blockages to money created by people:

    (a)   A customer goes into a shop and buys some goods worth Rs 400. He hands a 500 rupee note to the shopkeeper. The shopkeeper, thinking he was given a 1000 rupee note, gives the customer change of Rs 600. The customer, although aware of the mistake of the shopkeeper, feels happy about it and leaves the store with the money, thinking how stupid the man was. What he doesn't realize is that he has just sown the seed for one huge money block in his life.

(b) A young college boy travelling by bus manages to bypass paying the fare and thinks his cleverness saved him Rs 3. What he doesn't know is that he has blocked the flow of money into his life that could cost him a lot more than what he thought he saved, potentially amounting to Rs 30, or Rs 300, even Rs 30000. The flow of money is like a pipe that ceases to deliver water if it gets blocked by even a little pebble.

(c) A man was complaining to an acquaintance that someone had borrowed Rs 20000 from him and did not pay him back. For months, he repeatedly requested payment for the loan, but he was simply ignored. One day, this man asked his spiritual master for the solution to this problem. The master asked him whether he himself had withheld payment to someone. The man thought for a while and recalled how he had previously attended a course and did not pay the fees in full. The master nodded knowingly and advised him to go start paying the money, even if he had to do so in instalments of Rs 100 per month. The man agreed, and later was surprised that the person he loaned money to also began paying him in instalments. The flow of money had been opened both ways and the natural cycle was fulfilled. What's the moral of the story? To receive money, its inflow and outflow has to be kept constant without any forced blockages. To interfere with this flow is to go against the law of nature.

(5) Never Envy the Rich and the Successful

Many people make the mistake of envying or despising the rich and the successful. If you feel either way, you are in fact saying that you do not want to be rich. You block the road to success and prosperity that you have every right to receive. By praising the rich from your heart, you make friends with wealth, which then starts to work for you. If your neighbour wins a large sum of money in the lottery, congratulate and be happy for him instead of loathing him. In this way, richness ceases to keep its distance and eventually comes to you.

(6) Respect Money

It is commonly seen that people take their money lightly and don't bother to give it the respect it deserves. They roll, crumple, and mutilate bills and carelessly shove cash into their pockets or wallets. To respect money, you must handle it properly and keep it perfectly safe in a clean and orderly place. By observing these rules of thumb, you send out positive vibrations and energy attuned to money, which then flows into your life more abundantly.

Suppose you are travelling by a bus. You buy a ticket and the conductor gives you change that's fifty cents short. He tells you to collect the money before you get off. To some, fifty cents is negligible and they will just forget about it, while some will refuse to ask for it, thinking it's an embarrassingly small amount to want to get back. By not asking for what is rightfully yours, you disrespect money. So ask for your 50 cents! If the conductor honestly says he does not have the change yet by the time you reach your stop, then it's okay not to pursue any further. Just remember that asking for your own money is respecting it. So don't throw away money no matter how small it is. Money is meant to be used, but use it with the perfect understanding that it only serves to provide what you need to live in society. Possession of a large amount of money is not your ultimate goal.

(7) Do Not Think Negatively About Money

It's not right to merely focus on how much money has been spent for a purchase. This will only make you gripe. Your gain in the bargain must also be considered. When you spend Rs 500 on a shirt, do not focus on how much money you spent; instead focus on how you got a wonderful shirt in return for the payment. Always tell the whole truth to yourself. If you have spent money on a taxi instead of a bus, don't just fret about the extra cost, instead tell yourself how you had an easier and comfortable ride—avoiding the hassles of going shoulder-to-shoulder with other commuters in a packed ride. Avoiding any type of negativity about money is a simple technique to avoid negative financial programming of your subconscious mind. If you always say or feel that "My money is gone" every time you spend it, then your subconscious mind will accept it as a fact and will magnify that perception of "gone" many times over. But if you start focusing on what money brings into your life, then those things will be multiplied to your benefit.

(8) Money Flow Magical Technique

Whenever you hand money over to someone, feel it in your hands for a moment before letting it go. Say the following magical words: "This money is coming back to me in multiples. There is always enough." Feel the vibrations and the energy of the note, coin, cheque, or card between your fingers without giving in to any negative emotion. See how this technique alone can bring great results.

(9) Pray

The Circle of Money is ever present, so pray that you're included in this circle. Also pray that you can reach the perfect balance between materialism and spirituality. Pray with a strong faith. The best prayer is to ask that you be financially free so that you do not have to think about money at all.

(10) There Is No Money Problem, Just An Idea Problem

There is enough money to be made. All that is required is one creative idea. People lose their creative energy chasing money all their lives, but the truth is that there is no money problem—only the problem with getting ideas to make money. It's the right ideas that can help you create whatever fortune you want.

(11) Budgeting

Ask yourself these questions: What exactly happens to the income that I receive? Where and how was the money spent? Whatever answers you receive, note them down on a piece of paper or an account book. Your notes will give you a new direction. It will help you decide how and where your money should go in the future. Always be aware of where your money is going.

(12) Donate Wealth and Attain Happiness

Some think that when we donate or give money, our share of wealth decreases. That's not true. It is exactly the other way round. Money increases only when you start giving it. In fact, when you give, it comes back to you multiplied many times over.

Never think that you do not have anything to offer. If not money, you can give a helping hand to someone or you can simply wipe away someone's tears. A simple smile works like a charm and changes the mood and the thoughts of a sad person. Those who are open to giving whatever they have actually get more in return. The more money you give, the more money you will receive. However, it is important to take note of the value your donation has to the recipient and what it's to be used for. If you are charitable in the right way to the right person or cause, you will be well rewarded in return as is the way of nature.

YOUR CAREER — THE CORNERSTONE FOR FINANCIAL SUCCESS

Most of us associate a great career to financial success. A major part of our life is spent in our career. How we approach our career is the key to finding success in it. It should be as simple as studying in a school where you learn your lessons. However, most of us do not realize this and waste a lot of time overdoing things or dwelling on useless things, when all we need to do is answer a couple of questions: What lessons do I have to learn? Which lessons have I already learned? You should focus on these questions and let the answers guide your way towards the next step in learning new things in your career.

You can learn so many things in this school of life through your career. But where do you start? What follows are some lessons which will motivate and guide you in taking the next step in your career. These steps shall help you achieve success with your finances and every other aspect of your life.

First Lesson for a Successful Career: Cultivate Patience

Adversities teach patience in life

The very first lesson which you must learn is that adversities and problems in your career teach you about patience. It is important for everyone to know the virtues of patience. Therefore, make every adverse incident you experience an opportunity to learn patience.

Life is like a train. The moment you step on it, you experience some jolts. Though life is dynamic, but very often we get too "settled" in one place or situation, and refuse to move ahead. Nevertheless, life always tries to take us further by teaching us new lessons. The way it teaches us is just like how a train sometimes gives us a less than smooth ride as it starts and stops—pushing and nudging us until we get to where we're going.

Whenever life gives a push, people react in one of three ways, which helps in grouping them. The first group comprises of those who have thick skin, which means they are not affected by any jolt in life. They've lost their sensitivity after having gone through plenty of ups and downs, and fail to see what life is trying to teach them.

The second category consists of those who, after experiencing life's nudges, try to make life difficult for others. They treat other people in the same way they perceive life to be treating them. Whenever life tries to teach them anything by giving them a push, they get angry and vent this emotion on other people.

The third group is characterized by those who welcome all adversities with open arms. They consider life as a teacher and accept the lessons, no matter how painful, through those problems.

Thus, any problems or sudden changes that push you from your comfortable seat are really life's way of teaching you about... life. Knowing this, your reaction towards adversities and problems will change, wherever you may encounter them—at home or the workplace or the market. As your perspective changes, you stop reacting negatively every time life gives you a push—using situations or people. You cease to vent anger on other people and become more sensitive and patient towards them.

After taking in this first lesson, you will be surprised to realize that life's troubles are not what they appear to be. If you take adversities in stride, you will emerge from them a much stronger person.

Second Lesson for a Successful Career: Acquire Knowledge

Learn from others

Be attentive towards what others can offer you in terms of knowledge. Our eyes can see—so they tend to watch whatever comes in their field of vision—good or bad. We should learn to discipline our eyes and train them to focus on knowledge and to be ready to learn from everyone.

Life is like travelling on a train wherein there are three kinds of passengers you can meet. The first are those who have lots of money; second are those who have a great body; and third are those with a good stock of knowledge. Who should you focus on, given these kinds of people on the train? Is it the rich and fancy commuters, the good-looking people, or the wise ones? The truth is that you should not waste your time ogling at a beautiful body or on those dressed rich and fancy. These are trivial compared to the knowledgeable and wise. Setting sights on knowledge essentially leads you to people who can teach you something new. If your focus is on knowledge then you will attract everything that is necessary to lead a successful life. Hence, you should be inspired to learn from everyone.

If you happen to meet someone who has immense knowledge or wisdom, then make him your mentor for life, as you can always take good advice from him. With such a mentor, you will discover that your life is easier, simpler, and happier.

Third Lesson for a Successful Career: Be Fearless

Don't die a little death every day

The third lesson for a successful career is to learn to be fearless in life. Brave people can reach priceless treasures in life, whereas the cowardly nip their journey early on, thinking of all the troubles that may lie ahead. Such people tend to spend their entire life in fear and also die in fear.

In the train of life, there are certain people who spend their entire journey terrified and fearful—a "chicken" in colloquial terms. Now the third lesson states: "Never become a chicken nor ever listen to a chicken." This means you should not be fearful of trying out new things in life, no matter what people say. Breaking the mould requires a lot of courage, whereas repeating previous experiments is like sleep-walking through life. Being brave in life increases your courage and level of consciousness, which can lead to great financial success.

Scared people do not entertain courage. They run away just thinking about what scares them, like what the chicken did in this classic story.

In a forest, there was a chicken sitting under a mango tree, dreaming. Suddenly a mango fell from the tree onto a mound of dried leaves on the ground. The sound startled the chicken and she began shouting in fear, "The sky has fallen! The sky has fallen!" Upon hearing her frightened cries, the other animals, i.e. the Rabbit, Squirrel, Jackal, Deer, Elephant, Fox, and others, also began shouting and ran helter-skelter.

Lion, the king of the jungle, saw all the animals in their frenzy. "The sky has fallen! The sky has fallen!" they yelled. He couldn't understand the reason for this commotion, so he got hold of each of them and asked, "Where has the sky fallen?" But no one knew the answer as none of them had seen the sky falling. After some further enquiry, the lion found out about the chicken. Lion asked, "Where have you seen the sky falling?" The chicken replied, "I heard the sound of the sky falling." So Lion and all the animals went to the place where the chicken had heard the sound. There they discovered that it was a mango, and not the sky which had fallen. Fruits fall from trees all the time, but the sound of the falling mango scared the chicken so much that she thought that it was a piece of the sky and spread the scare throughout the jungle.

In real life too, there are people who are just like the chicken and spread fear among others for no reason at all.

With the help of the story, you come to realize how people can be like a chicken. As you ride the train of life, you come across many chickens that spread their fear in people around them. They will always tell you that the sky will fall whenever you take an unconventional step. For them, every new undertaking means inviting failure. Do you remember, when you were a kid you tried hundreds of new things every day like a curious cat? Now that you're an adult, do you act more like a chicken than a curious cat? Cats can reach places a hen can never reach; likewise you have to be fearless in order to reach goals in your life. They say curiosity kills the cat, but then again, they also say a cat has nine lives. So stop being afraid.

Fourth Lesson for a Successful Career: Listen to Your Heart

Live your life like an open book

The fourth lesson for a successful career teaches how to keep playing in the field, to rise above the ordinary, and to be open to others. Those who live a selfish life and purposely avoid interacting and communicating with others, are like a closed book, unwelcoming and distant. On the rare occasions they do interact with others, they may do one of two things—either criticize or be suspicious of them. This type of people is characterized by a tendency to belittle others, and it's as if they're telling people, "You don't have the brains to amount to anything in life." They emphasize the negative traits of others, while ignoring the positive ones. They are cunning in their dealings by how they manipulate facts.

You do not have to be like a closed book and be dead to others, so don't listen to these people as they will only criticize what you do and also what you don't do! They will suck the life out of you until you're either nothing but a shell of your former self or you become like them. The good news is you have a choice. You don't have to turn into the kind of person that you despise. Therefore, apply the knowledge you have gained from this book and give importance to what your heart says. Opening your heart opens up your intellect. Proper use of the head and the heart is a sure formula for success. It pays to use intuition based on complete knowledge.

Fifth Lesson for a Successful Career: Be Alert

Break your mechanical habits

The fifth lesson is on being alert and conscious about yourself and your surroundings. Do not live like a lifeless machine that only goes through the motions without living the moment. Avoid being a slave to mechanical habits and going through life as if sleepwalking.

Today, more than 90 percent of people live their life like a machine. They are not living life as human beings should and would rather behave mechanically, following a pattern of activities that repeat, day in and day out. Most people actually live this kind of mechanical life with prescribed transitions—they grow up, they go to school, they graduate, they work, they get married, they have children, they raise their children, they become grandparents, and then they die.

Ask yourself the question: Is this what you call life? Is this the only aim of life, or are there other bigger aims which need to be achieved? To break from set patterns is the ultimate aim of life, by which you make your mind pure.

Mechanical living involves people reacting in the same way as they always have to a particular situation or incident. If someone curses them, for example, they get angry and curse in return. If anyone praises them, they smile and feel proud. Throughout the day, people act like a machine programmed to do only certain things, and if they happen to be told the fact that they are leading a robotic life, they get angry, which in effect, is an affirmation of the set patterns characterized by programmed or "mechanical" behaviour. Such people are never ready to learn anything new in life. They live life criticizing and suspecting others of things that they only imagine. If you fall into this category and wish to break free from your machine-like behaviour, then you must promise yourself, or better yet, take a vow, not to fall into set stereotypical patterns. If you have always been suspicious of others, for example, stop!

People who act like machines behave according to beliefs and lifestyles that have been instilled in them. We see plenty of these machines around us—some of them belong to the zodiac sign Aries, some Taurus, some Scorpio, and so on. These machines behave in exactly the same manner as their future has been predicted. Even a cheap newspaper can forecast their life since they always behave in the same manner. What's important to them is getting by every day—to eat, sleep, and have a good time. They are not aware of their actual aim in life and "exist" just for the sake of it. They are always in trouble and in turn trouble others. They often become a burden to society, never knowing how it is to really live as a boon to society. They will likely die as they have lived—without purpose. Hence it is very important to come out of the mould of your beliefs and notions to live life the right way.

People can snap out of their machine-like existence the moment they realize they are living like a machine. This realization is very important. Once they know that they've become like robots, they can then make a real effort to change their patterns and truly start living for the first time.

Palm-readers foretell an individual's future; he believes it and starts living his life accordingly. He changes his plans for the day based on what astrologers say regarding his horoscope. He becomes totally dependent on his so-called fate. Thus, people who believe in astrology, zodiac signs, and the stars, get entangled in false beliefs and notions. They do not realize that a prediction foretells only one possibility in a person's future, whereas the reality is that there are infinite possibilities. And it's a fact that a person can choose the possibility he desires. But if he unaware of this fact, he is then influenced into believing what astrologers tell him. When Gautam Buddha was born, various astrologers said that he will become a mighty king. But there was only one learned person who said that he had the possibility of becoming either a mighty king or an enlightened soul. Both of these things proved to be correct in their own way.

Similarly, there are infinite possibilities for each and every one. But a person gets bogged down by what's been read or told about a possible future event in his life. If someone, for instance, tells him that his day will not go well, he may get so bothered by it that his day actually turns out to be like what he thought it would be—all based on information that was fed to him by someone who really didn't know any better.

A person who doesn't care about his future can become stuck in patterns of useless behaviour, such that he (or she) can become so habituated to doing something—like watching television in the evenings after work—that he will continue to do that for the rest of his life without ever having any goals or direction other than to turn on the TV and watch shows until it's time to sleep. Nothing new ever happens in his life with this kind of habit. If you want to break out of a useless existence, then it's important that you get out of the set patterns of unproductive behaviour. Otherwise, you will not be able to do anything new or become a better person.

It was said that a boy would become enlightened and be free from the rigours of fate and luck; that his life will not be dependent on the lines of his palms, which meant that he will live an enlightened life and not a mechanical one. That boy became the Buddha. You may not know it, but you also have a budding Buddha inside of you waiting to be realized. Like the Buddha, you too can be free from a life that's more of a machine's than a human being's. Once you pull yourself out of your personal rut, nothing can stop you from becoming successful since you will then be able to explore all the possibilities that lie hidden within you.

Sixth Lesson for a Successful Career: Acquire Wisdom

Wisdom, not money, is everything

The sixth lesson is on elevating the level of your wisdom. People spend their entire lives earning money instead of enhancing their wisdom. Today, success is measured in terms of money. Everywhere around you, people have made huge buildings, various facilities, and endless means of entertainment with the help of money. A misconception has developed that money is everything in life. Anyone who has lots of money is called successful. But success does not really come with money; it comes with knowledge and wisdom. Money comes only after you acquire wisdom, which includes knowing how to make money.

You will realize this only if you cease to live like a machine that is programmed to run after money. If you have knowledge and wisdom, you will easily get money. As has been discussed before, 90 percent of people who win a lottery revert to their original condition after squandering all the prize money. It's a fact that only the remaining 10 percent can make wise use of their money. The reason for this is that the 90 percent do not have control over their mind and body.

If anyone says that he can buy brains with money, he should know that to do so, he should have brains in the first place.

Seventh Lesson for a Successful Career: Exercise Self-Control

Have control over your body and mind

Animals do not have to live a disciplined life; only humans have to do so because they unconsciously start living a mechanical life. Wild animals never seem to suffer from diseases like diabetes or hypertension because they lead a very simple life. Whenever they feel hungry, they eat, and only just enough of what is required for them to live. But humans, in spite of being told not to consume too much sugar because of the risk of diabetes, just cannot resist the temptation. This happens because humans do not have control over their bodies. So, in spite of the knowledge that smoking and alcohol are harmful for the lungs and the liver respectively, people keep on making and consuming cigarettes and strong alcoholic beverages. Again, the reason is because humans do not have enough control over their body and mind. For the most part, people are controlled by the cravings of the body, which are fundamental to addiction. The result is a cycle of finding excuses and gratification of undesirable habits.

You can start rising from such habitual follies if you do away with even a small aspect of your mechanical existence. Shun all the bad habits starting today and make a commitment to stay away from them. Only then can you achieve and maintain success in your life.

Eighth Lesson for a Successful Career: Progress

Mantra for progress: Always win

Life always wants progress. The mantra of progress is: "Always win." If you make sure that you never lose to failure, then you will always win. You will realize the value of this mantra when you learn that losing to anything is not a failure; rather, it's losing to failure that is the true failure.

After losing to something, the tendency is to get scared, and that is when you actually lose. Some people lose only because of fear of failure. The fear that comes after failure is actually responsible for more failures later on. Therefore, it makes sense not to lose to failure. This can be done if you do not get scared of failure and do not stop trying to succeed. If you do this when faced with failure, then you will not lose anything. Such a reaction to failure is actually a motivation for winning, so you should take it as a sign to move on with your sights still set on winning.

Always remember the mantra of progress. Once you have stopped losing to failure, you will never get scared of failure, which only becomes like a stepping stone for success in life. Successful people will tell you that they too have had many failures in their life, but unlike the unsuccessful ones, they never dwelt on them. They always looked ahead and focused on solving the problems identified in order to be successful. When a child is eagerly learning to ride a bicycle, falling down is a given. But being bent on learning how to ride, the child merely brushes the falls aside, thinking nothing of them. The child's focus is on learning to ride the bicycle because he sees in his mind how fun it would be. He pictures himself riding the bicycle just like the other children. Even a child knows how to focus on succeeding, and therefore learns things, like riding a bicycle, quickly even with the scrapes that go with it. As a child grows into adulthood, however, the mind slowly becomes conditioned into needless self-preservation mode because of the hurts experienced with failure that become etched in memory. Fear is the result which prevents people from being able to learn to ride "new bicycles" in their lives.

People who habitually succeed have placed the anticipation of success over programmed fears ingrained while growing up, so they never get worried of falling down; and if they do fall down, they simply learn from it and make their odds better for succeeding. They make sure the same mistakes don't happen again.

Ninth Lesson for a Successful Career: Forget Your Fears

Take calculated risks

If you want to achieve major successes in life, then it is necessary to take risks. Those who always want to be on the safe side never achieve big success. Always remember the motto of successful people: "If you are scared of taking a risk, then take it immediately." Ask yourself: Is the happiness that comes after success more than my fear of failure? If the answer is "yes," then it follows that you can face any challenge in life. However, if the fear of failure is greater than your anticipation of happiness, then go through the tenth lesson of life and learn how to make a powerful goal that overpowers hindrances to success.

You should take well-calculated risks in life, although in taking these risks, you have to face lots of fears that you must get rid of to build courage in yourself. Don't be scared of taking well-measured risks, which are different from reckless risks.

If you get scared to go to the bathroom late at night because you think it's so dark, then don't wait for the fear to get the upper hand and take control of the situation. The moment you get thoughts of fear, just quickly do what you need to do, may it be going to the bathroom or making a speech in front of an audience. It is very important to take risks, because for the most part, the fears are actually unfounded in real life and are merely by-products of your mind's tendency for overprotection or wrong programming of your mind. Nevertheless, taking risks should be well-calculated because those who take risks without prior thought end up facing heavy consequences for their brash actions. That's usually the case in gambling. But taking action on limited risks will make you brave, and at the same time give you better chances of winning.

Tenth Lesson for a Successful Career: Have a Sense of Direction

Have a powerful goal in life

Have a powerful goal in life. How many people make a goal for themselves in life and how many of them note it down? Remembering your goal in life is important, for as long as you are not reminded of your goal, you continue leading your life in the same way as before. If you are asked about your goal in life, what will you answer? If you have not set a goal, then make one and try to fulfil it. And if you already have a goal, then strive to make it more powerful. With a set goal, you instinctively address all the problems that come in the way of fulfilling it. Without a goal to reach, every little problem will seem to be a huge burden.

Without a goal in life, you will be weighted by obstacles at every step. But if you have a well-defined goal, problems will disappear even before they make their presence felt. Give yourself a powerful goal which makes you feel happy just thinking about it and excites you such that you want to achieve it at any cost.

Give your life an aim. Don't wait for the right circumstances or for someone to come and tell you your aim in life. No one knows you better than yourself, so you shouldn't be dependent on the opinion of others. Try to define an aim for your life on your own. Consider the day you find your aim as the most wonderful one of your life. It's because on that day, you have identified an aim that will give direction to your life. This direction will lead to your growth.

The bigger our aim, the more energy nature provides us to achieve it. People who understand this rule of nature are never satisfied with a small aim. So, if you want to feel the strength of nature in you, make your aim in life a lofty one.

Eleventh Lesson for a Successful Career: Learn to Give

Become instrumental for others

The eleventh lesson teaches us that whatever we want to achieve, we must help others in achieving it. This is a sure-shot method to attain what you desire because it is a rule of nature that whatever you give unselfishly to others will come back to you multiplied many times.

Someone might say, "People don't seem to be happy to meet me and can't even force a smile when talking to me." He should be told: "To get people to smile and be happy with you around, you have to smile first; only then will they start smiling back at you." When you start smiling around people, you will discover that after some time, everyone around you will be smiling back. If you want people to be nice and say "hello" to you, then you must take the initiative and say hello to those who you meet. You will see that these same people will start smiling and be nice to you in just a few days. You might be amazed at how easy it is to make people reciprocate your greetings.

We generally feel that we will start giving something only after we have received it. It seems natural, but that is not correct. Whatever you want, first try to give that to others. What if all people only waited for others to give something good to them? There has to be someone who will give first. Will a man who comes home to his cabin during a cold winter night get warmth if he demands the fireplace to first give him warmth and only then he will give wood and a flame to it? The same principle works in life. You must first learn to give to others for you to receive. If you want to receive money, then help others to earn money. Similarly, if you want to gain knowledge, then help others to gain it first. If you want to have time, then give time to others or help others in managing or saving their time. If you want to get love from people, then love them first, or help them to be loved.

When you become instrumental in helping someone to achieve something, you will be amazed to receive what you selflessly gave away, many times over.

Twelfth Lesson for a Successful Career: Harbour Hope Always

Become optimistic and give importance to positive thoughts

The twelfth lesson of life can be understood through an ancient example. You may have heard of the story of Mahabharata wherein a battlefield is described with Arjuna standing between the warring sides—the Pandavas and the Kauravas. Arjuna represents the "I", "Me," or "Myself" within an individual. The Pandavas, who are on one side of the battleground, represent a person's positive thoughts. On the other side there are the Kauravas, and they represent the negative thoughts. In the epic, the Kauravas outnumber the Pandavas a hundred to five warriors. This lopsided ratio actually reflects the fact that people usually harbour more of negative thoughts rather than positive ones.

In the middle of the battlefield, Arjuna is at a loss on what to do. He is surrounded by negative thoughts. The one who guides him is Lord Krishna, a symbol of wisdom, who tells him to fire towards his adversary, the Kauravas. The lesson here is that whenever negative thoughts dominate, never stop firing and to fire according to your understanding, which may be improved by thinking of the truth. The moment you start thinking of the truth (what needs to be done given the circumstances), negative thoughts vanish.

Weigh the negative thoughts against the positive thoughts within you. If the negative thoughts significantly outweigh the positive thoughts, you can easily do away with the negative thoughts with what you know to be true and finish them off. If negative thoughts are equal to positive thoughts, you can easily use them to your advantage by using them as a stepping stone to progress. Allow them to motivate you to reach what you're aiming for. In a sense, Arjuna was told to finish off all the negative thoughts. Now, you may not have the voice of heaven giving you commands right into your ear, but the thing is that whenever you think that you are not able to do something, ask yourself how you can actually do it. You will get the answer and thus you will overcome the negative thinking. Those who harbour positive thoughts need only think about how they can complete the task and go ahead with it.

Negative thoughts obstruct your progress. Remove those obstacles with the help of positive thoughts and move ahead towards your goal. Always be positive while doing something new. Remember that you are the child of God and hence your success is confirmed. When you have positive thoughts, your brain starts working overtime in order to help you to achieve your aim. Negative thoughts pull you back.

When you say, "I can't do this," you stamp a question mark on your brain. But you think optimistically when you ask instead, "What must I do to complete this work?" This way, you give your brain an opportunity to think. Your brain will open new vistas for you and, as a consequence, it will develop further. If you wish to purchase something and you think you can't make enough money for it, simply stop thinking that way and instead say to yourself, "What can I do to earn enough money to buy this thing?" This way, you open up a pathway wherein lies the means and the opportunity to buy your prized item.

Thirteenth Lesson for a Successful Life: From "Mine" to "Yours"

Try to discover life in you as you remove the thought of 'I'

The last lesson for a great career is to have an impersonal vision. An example of a personal vision is what's epitomized by the statement: "I shall be CEO of my own company one day." On the other hand, an impersonal vision is typified by the thoughts of what you can do for others, like when you know with a certainty that you can provide jobs to so many thousands of people or usher in a new technology that will change the world. Your vision of teaching, for example, is personal if your aim is to become a famous academician. But it is impersonal if your goal is to make a positive impact on the lives of thousands of students.

Your career takes a fantastic turn for the better once you identify your impersonal vision associated with it and then pursue it. Then money and finances become just vehicles and mediums that support the attainment of your impersonal vision.

This last lesson for success teaches you to be free from thoughts with selfish pronouns like "I," "me," and "myself." The moment you become free from these words, you achieve a life that is also free of the cycle of birth and death. Learning this lesson is where you undertake the journey from "Mine" to "Yours." Here's an analogy wherein you can get a deeper understanding of this journey.

When parents leave their children at home for some days, how do the children spend this time? Depending on the nature of their children, the parents provide some things to them before leaving. They give a radio to the children who like listening to music. Some of the kids like to watch movies, so they are provided with a video. Some of the kids are given a Ludo to play with, which is a simple board game. In this manner, different games are given to different children while they are at home by themselves.

When the parents come back, what condition of the children will make them happy and what will make them sad? Obviously, on returning home if they find their children crying, they too will become sad. On the other hand, if they find their children content and enjoying themselves, they will feel good.

In this example you can see how you yourself are like a child left on Earth by God for some time (life span). Like everyone else, you actually fall under one of six types of children of God.

Are you the type usually found to be unconscious? This first category of children includes the ones who have spent much of their life smoking, drinking, and taking drugs. Seeing them in this condition, their parents would definitely feel very sad.

The second category of children includes the ones who have done major damage at home. They have broken all the toys given to them as well as the furniture of the house. Parents feel very sad to find their children in this state.

The third category of children is characterized by those who often cry and are generally miserable. Parents feel bad to see their children way looking so distraught, having spent all their time crying.

No parent will feel proud of these three categories of children. But fortunately, there are three other categories of children that are quite the opposite and will surely make their parents proud.

The fourth category comprises of children who are thankful to their parents and immediately run and hug them because they had a fantastic time while left at home.

Children of the fifth category are those who are not only happy themselves but also have made other children in the house happy. They have taken good care of them and assured them that mom and dad will be coming back soon.

Children of the sixth category are the happiest and have a wide influence that reaches beyond the house into the neighbourhood, making children in other houses happy as well. Moreover, they have been responsible enough to clean their home and throw out all the garbage. They have managed the house very well. They are the ones who managed to breach the confines of their otherwise mechanical life and attained self-realization or enlightenment. Parents feel very happy and proud of such children and live with them ever after.

Those children who cry in discontent are the ones who are given a prize in the form of a handkerchief to wipe their tears. Until they learn how to live and take control of their life, their parents are going to give them the same reward, and they will be wiping their tears for as long as they don't grow up.

Life that sustains us, and that which we also call God, is within ourselves. We all have the feeling of being alive inside of us. This is reinforced when our parents (God) begin to live with us. Most people know of only one life, but there is actually another kind of life called Supreme Life. In life, there is death, but there is no death associated with the Supreme Life. To live with this understanding is the thirteenth lesson of life, in which the word "Mine" is superseded by the word "Yours," which means acknowledgement that everything belongs to God.

Desires are not obstacles as long as they are not attached with the word "Me." When desires become "my desires" then they convert into the cause of sorrow. To have desires is not bad in itself, but to get attached to them is wrong. Liberate yourself from the cycle of "I," "Me," and "Mine," to be able to achieve ultimate success.

Summary of the thirteen lessons for a successful career and a successful life:

Lesson number	Lesson name	Purpose of lesson
(1)	Cultivate patience	Life teaches lessons by giving troubles. It is very important for everyone on this Earth to learn patience. Hence consider every incident in life as an opportunity for increasing patience.
(2)	Acquire knowledge	Develop discipline of your eyes. Your eyes can see, so they watch everything that comes across. You should train your eyes to focus on acquiring knowledge. Be ready to learn things from everyone and everything.
(3)	Be fearless	Brave people can attain the hidden treasure of life. A scared person only thinks of the troubles ahead and terminates his journey. Such people spend their entire lives in fear and even die with fear.
(4)	Listen to your heart	Try to work according to whatever knowledge you have acquired. People will always criticize you whether you do something or not. Listen to your heart and give importance to the feelings of your heart.

(5)	Be alert	Always be aware and alert. Unconscious people, or those living in a sleep-like state, waste their entire lives doing nothing. Their life is meaningless.
(6)	Acquire wisdom	Raise your level of wisdom. People, instead of acquiring wisdom, waste their entire lives in earning money. You cannot buy wisdom with all the money in the world if you do not have wisdom to start with.
(7)	Exercise self-control	Learn to discipline your mind and body if you do not want to live like a machine.
(8)	Progress	The mantra for progress is "Always win." You can never lose if you don't allow yourself to be defeated by failure.
(9)	Forget your fears	If you want to achieve success in life, then it is important to take calculated risks. Those who always want to be safe will never achieve major success.
(10)	Make a powerful goal	Always have a clear and powerful aim in life. Very few people aim for something in their life and fewer note it down so they don't forget. Until you remind yourself daily of your aim, you will keep on living the same kind of life that you always have.

(11)	Learn to give	Help others to achieve what you've always wanted to in life. Whatever you give to others, you get it back multiplied many times over.
(12)	Have a positive outlook	Whenever you think that you cannot accomplish a task, think positive thoughts. Instead of saying, "I cannot accomplish this task," say, "What can I do so that I can accomplish it?"
(13)	Move from "Mine" to "Yours"	To help you achieve Supreme Life that is free of death, just get rid of words like "I," "My," and "Mine." Do so by cultivating an impersonal vision and pursuing it by helping others.

Financial Transformation Action Plan

(1) _____

(2) _____

(3) _____

(4) _____

(5) _____

(6) _____

(7) _____

(8) _____

(9) _____

(10) _____

(11) _____

(12) _____

(13) _____

(14) _____

(15) _____

(16) _____

(17) _____

(18) _____

(19) _____

(20) _____

Part 6

Social Transformation: Encounter with the Heart

THREE MAGICAL STEPS TOWARDS GOOD HUMAN RELATIONS

Three Magical Steps

You can either motivate others or inspire others. They're two different things. Motivation is an external pressure using the other person's fear or greed. Inspiration, on the other hand, comes from within. In other words, the desire to do something comes from within, which is apart from any external suggestions.

It is important to learn how to deal with others, how you should get work done, and how you can prove to be helpful in inspiring others.

Those, who do not have self-confidence and fail to know how to deal with people, fail in their lives as well. Thus, it is important to undergo social transformation, i.e., knowing how to inspire, interact, and work with people. For transformation to occur at the social level, you must learn the following three magical steps:

Magical Step No. 1:   Observation (for you)

Magical Step No. 2:   Appreciation (for others)

Magical Step No. 3:   Be a good news reporter (for the world)

Magical Step No. 1
We become what we observe

Everyone observes, but what do people observe, really? If you haven't noticed, most people observe only the imperfections and shortfalls of others. They effortlessly point out what's the problem with others and readily describe their shortcomings and vices. They preoccupy themselves in observing the negative aspects of those around them and some even get a kick out of it. So like everyone else, these people do observe, but they observe exactly those things which they don't need in their lives. The first magical step or rule is to know that you get or become what you observe. Hence, you have to learn to keep your antennae pointed in the right direction.

A baby learns to do a number of things such as walking, talking, and playing only by observing other people. Therefore, one must understand the significance of observation in learning.

The significance of observation

An astonishing fact is that an ordinary human being observes only a thousandth part of what he sees. Yet, he is capable of learning and imitating, if he wants to, whatever he observes. If you are interested in measuring your capacity for observation, then pause for a while and test yourself through the following experiment. Ask yourself the questions that follow and soon you will learn about the level of your observation skills.

(1) Take a plain piece of paper. Start writing about the watch you are wearing without looking at the watch. (If you don't have a watch, then use some other object that you use regularly.) Recollect and write about the colour of the dial, and the style and colour of the numbers on the face. Does it have any jewels, if so, how many? What is its brand name? What kind of border does it have? In this activity, you can check how familiar you are with your own watch or whatever item you have chosen. It will reveal how good

your power of observation is.

(2) Try to remember the details of the lane or road you have been using for years. Mentally observe and make a note of it keeping in mind every turn, bump, and corner shop. You will be surprised to note many things which you have not consciously noticed before.

Observation is the greatest instrument

The human race has received the capability for observation as its greatest instrument, a gift, which is always functioning. Because of your ability to observe, you will always be registering things in your memory and you are bound to use them. In order to understand this in detail, take a look at the following examples:

(1) Your friend is singing a song. Later in the day, you find yourself singing the same song.

(2) If you are impressed by the way a film star walks, you keenly observe his movement, and later, you too start walking in the same style even without practising.

(3) You don't tell jokes, but your new friend is fond of telling them. The two of you spend a lot of time together and soon you develop the same habit.

(4) As a child, you see your mother gesturing while talking. As you grow up, you develop the same habit even without trying. Children do tend to adopt their parents' mannerisms because they observe them very closely.

Try to understand through these examples how people develop habits; how they import various habits of others into their persona. It means all the things and habits that you are observing have the capability to shape you, even if you do not like them. What you observe tends to stick with you, be it good or bad. The mind is like a camera. It makes an imprint of whatever it sees. Thus, be cautious when observing and focus only on the things that you want, and ignore those that you do not wish to have.

It makes sense to choose the company that suits your needs, because only in the right company can you observe what you want to use or wish to become. If you wish to be a trader, then be in the company of traders, not technicians! If you wish to be a lawyer, then be in the presence of lawyers, not doctors! If you wish to be a musician, then be in tune with singers and composers, not beauticians! You want to be a teacher? Then, adopt the company of great teachers and also listen to what the gurus have to say and follow their example! Want to be a champion in sports? Then, rub shoulders with the winners and title holders.

As a result of what you absorb through observation, you can easily attain the kind of success that you have set as a goal for yourself. However, if you are climbing a mountain, be careful not to join hands with those who are climbing down, or you too may feel like going down, even before you should. It is human nature to pick up negative ways faster. Therefore, always focus on what you have set your mind to achieve. By taking the first step, you will easily develop within yourself positive qualities and also learn the art of taking interest in the good that you see in others. Additionally, careful observation will steady your focus on what you're aiming for in life. Thus, it can safely be inferred that you receive not what you think you deserve, but rather what you observe. Once you've mastered the correct way to observe, you become ready for the second magical step.

Magical Step No. 2
Appreciate others generously with purity of mind.

Don't criticize; critiguide instead.

The first magical step was for your benefit. This second step is for others' benefit. Do not be afraid to express appreciation for the good qualities you observe in others. It will cost you nothing.

However, you should give only good and sincere appreciation. Also, do not limit your appreciation to just your loved ones. There are people around who are rich in qualities, which can be as basic as good handwriting skills or as bizarre as a talent in a sport like cup stacking. It may not be obvious at first, but some people you meet may really be good musicians, painters, or philanthropists. You need to appreciate the good qualities of all such people. Hence, when you change your outlook and begin to focus only on the positive qualities of others, you will develop good relationships on top of good observation skills. Whenever you come across a person, ask yourself, "What do I like about him?" and start thinking about his good qualities. Is it his smile, a good dressing sense, good behaviour, cleanliness, frankness, intelligence, or the manner of talking?

When interacting with others, it is wise to state the good qualities you like about them. At such moments, you subconsciously express your liking to the other person. Consequently, that person will start liking you in return, and your interaction with him will become livelier, improving your social relation with him as a result. Here you can see how magical the tool of appreciation can be. It is the white magic of human engineering and works in all relationships. Who doesn't like a compliment or two? Appreciation makes a person feel important and liked. Unfortunately, people almost never use this white magic since they are too busy being critical of others, arguing to prove them wrong. Nothing tramples down on a person more than destructive criticism. It's one of the reasons why employees call it quits; they do not leave companies—they leave their criticizing managers.

Therefore, always be generous in appreciating others. Whenever you get an opportunity to appreciate someone, grab it. You should be the first to appreciate others and the last one to criticize. Learn the art of critiguiding. If the subject is about food, for example, it makes no difference if you choose to mention, or not, the need for more salt in food or more sugar in a cup of tea, because your host, too, will be having the same food or tea. If you really need to say something, then compliment your host about the food served! Sometimes, saying nothing says everything. Always be careful with what you say to others. Rude and harsh words always remain in memory.

It is wrong to assume that by criticizing others, you can improve them. Nobody likes to be criticized. Ask yourself how you feel when someone criticizes you and how you feel when somebody appreciates you. Do not criticize people. They are just the way you would be if you were under similar circumstances. Criticizing only makes the other person more resentful and unnecessarily creates more enemies for you. It's one way you make someone feel inferior and unimportant. By criticizing, you only try to prove the other person wrong. Knowingly or unknowingly you hurt feelings and spoil your relationship with the person, the consequences of which stay with you in the long run.

Hitler, straight from childhood, received only criticism. He took out his resentment by waging a war on other people and torturing them in concentration camps. It has been seen in most cases that daughters-in-law who get censured and abused by their mothers-in-law, give the same treatment to their daughters-in-law. In some places, it can be a vicious cycle that continues down generations. People who have been degraded a lot do not rest until they take out their resentment on others in situations similar to what they went through. Thus, a child, who was brought up by a strict father, grows up and treats his own children in the same way.

For social transformation to take place, you are required to break this pattern of criticism. It is like the popular English game, Pass the Parcel, wherein everybody wants to give the parcel to somebody else. Criticism is just like that. No one likes it. The simple solution is to ban criticism from your life. Criticism is destructive and can break relationships, families, friendships, hearts, and homes.

Critiguide

If you do need to give negative feedback, then do not criticize, instead, critiguide. Use the sandwich formula: Bread on both sides and the spicy stuff in between. This means you should first appreciate the person about the right things that he has done; and then, very subtly, and in a friendly tone, guide him in the areas which require improvement. Consequently, you help him get the work done and you keep a friend.

It is necessary to understand that you cannot achieve success in life without the help of others. If you aim for something high, you need the support of many hands, and this can be achieved not by criticism, but by appreciation. When you can get work done using sweet words, then why use harsh words? When honey will do, why use poison? People itch to pick others apart and feel happy to point their faults. That's easy, but that doesn't mean it's right or useful.

There are several ways of critiguiding which can be mastered by you

How does a doctor treat a patient? He listens to what the patient has to say, then, very softly and with genuine care, he tells him, "There's nothing to worry about because you will soon be well. It's just a minor problem, so don't be afraid." This said, the patient recovers within a few days. The doctor may prescribe bitter pills to swallow, but his words are sugar-coated. If you have to throw something bitter to somebody, then, say something sweet to him as well. If you need to scold someone, then before doing so, appreciate the good qualities of that person.

Encouragement works faster

Everything depends on how you encourage people. Remember the million dollar questions: "What's in it for them?" and "Why will they want to help you?" They will not be interested in listening to anything that is linked with your personal gains, so clarify the gains they will receive. Talk of what is beneficial for them and they will be happy to walk your talk.

Don't be a critic, but welcome the critics

By now it's clear that it's a bad idea to criticize others. On the other hand, if you come across a critic who starts counting your mistakes, there is no need to argue with him. Instead you should listen to him carefully and patiently with the attitude that this man is only trying to help you become a better person. This attitude will be really beneficial.

Here's a story. A painter shows his painting to his friend, who is also a painter. The friend points out several mistakes in the painting. The painter does not feel hurt at all and he listens as his mistakes are pointed out and takes them in stride, remembering them so that he doesn't make the same mistakes again. He actually applies the suggestions in another painting, and goes back to his friend to show his work. The friend again finds several faults with the painting and the painter just goes back and corrects them. As a result, the painter keeps on improving his painting, making each new work more beautiful than the last one. It doesn't take long before he becomes a world famous artist. In like manner, if you welcome the comments of critics and listen to their criticism, then you actually help yourself improve.

Magical Step No. 3

Be a Good News Reporter (GNR)

The first magical step benefits you. The second one benefits others near you. This third magical step will actually benefit everybody. It's when you become a GNR or Good News Reporter. When you read a newspaper in the morning, the news about the entire world is literally on your table. News of murders, smuggling, kidnapping, thefts, and terrorism catch your eye. You carry the news that shock you and discuss them with others who give their own opinion about it. This happens several times and by the end of the day, you're overwhelmed by depressing news.

But now you can make a small change. As soon as you get the newspaper tomorrow, you can concentrate on the good news, like a story about a genius inventing an engine that counters global warming, or an article about a countryman awarded a gold medal in the Olympics. It doesn't have to be big news always. It can be as small as a kid rescuing a kitten from being run over, or a taxi driver returning a wallet full of money to the rightful owner, or a charitable trust organizing a free health camp. Any news will do as long as it makes you feel good.

Be a GNR and talk about good news to your friends, and in turn, they will give you good news and other happy stories, some of which may not even be in the newspapers. Like attracts like, so good news attracts more good news.

It is interesting to note that if you extend a bit of good news, in return you receive two bits of good news. Extended further this can trigger a chain of ever-increasing good news. There is another aspect of news multiplication. When two people listen to you about some good news, then it is passed on to four other people; from four people, it spreads to eight; and from eight, it gets heard by sixteen… You got the idea. Towards the end of the day, the news is passed on to millions of people. On the Internet, it's called the viral effect. Your little initiative will spread a growing wave of happiness among people everywhere. Thus, there is no doubt that one person—that's you—can change the whole world.

People will start to eagerly wait for you in order to receive some good news, because they know that only you can make them feel happy in spite of all the bad news floating around. Due to your jolly attitude, even your family members will wait for you to give a good report, tell a few jokes, and narrate some feel-good stories. If you present yourself in this manner at home and in public, you can make everybody happy. Therefore, become a GNR.

The best way to be a GNR is to laugh heartily with others and spread happy thoughts through laughter. A smiling person is naturally a friendly person and is liked by everybody. The one who cries, cries alone. If you have the desire to win the hearts of people, then learn to smile and laugh.

Today, it would seem that people need a reason to laugh. Water is wet by nature, not by reason. Likewise, laughter is human nature – you don't need a reason to laugh. Have you ever seen dry water? But you must have certainly come across people who don't laugh. It's really their choice.

Laughter is a universal language. Laughter is at the core of every human being and it comes instinctively. Nobody teaches a baby to laugh. It laughs on its own whenever it feels like it. If a baby needs no cause to laugh, you too should understand that laughing is part of being human, and the more people practise it, the more real is the prospect for social transformation.

So we laugh! We may have laughed so many times, but have we ever heard ourselves laugh? So stop reading the book for a while and laugh loudly for a minute (if you are alone) and listen to your laughter. Concentrate on it. Feel it well up inside of you and get released vocally.

Whenever you get an opportunity to laugh, listen to your laughter. It is the law of nature that whatever you give attention to grows. Where attention goes, energy also flows. So the more you focus on your laughter, the more it will grow. In this way, you will make yourself happy and spread happiness to others as well.

THE SEVEN LEVELS OF RELATIONSHIPS

Have you ever thought over the meaning and the nature of a relationship? How many of us have explored the multiple dimensions of a relationship, or pondered as to why we are often compelled to relate the way we do? Let us explore the answers to some of these questions and understand how we can bring our relationships to a higher level. There are seven levels of relationships. Let us try to understand each one using the husband-wife relationship as an example.

First Level

The first level is characterized by the frequent petty quarrels between the husband and the wife which, most often, end up in big fights, making each of them feel that marriage is all about fighting. At this level of consciousness, what matters is winning or having the last word. Imagine what the world will be like if such couples raise their children in such an environment.

Second Level

At the second level, the couple becomes aware that they are constantly fighting and it's not normal. They also begin to realize the reasons why they fight in the first place. This is, of course, an improvement from the first level since things become clearer and the relationship starts to get ironed out.

Third Level

At the third level, the husband and the wife begin to understand not only the cause of their fights, but also try to find solutions to their problems together. The husband now starts to see things from the wife's point of view and vice versa. He thinks it would have been different if he had given her flowers or if he had come home in time for dinner. The wife also starts to figure out that she could have served the food with much more grace instead of just dumping it on his plate. She recognizes that the situation would have been better if she had not thrown a tantrum or had not acted intimidating. Now they identify the reasons for their disagreements and try to avoid these by amending their own behaviour. This realization and willingness to compromise and be more understanding takes them to the next level.

Fourth Level

At this level, they begin to dig deep into the real reasons behind their conflicts. They realize that on the surface, they may be arguing about the same familiar issues (time, money, responsibility, and so forth), but unconsciously, their arguments are caused by other less obvious reasons. The wife recognizes that she is not upset because he came home late for dinner; what actually upset her is some past unsettled matter, and his coming in late merely triggered her anger. There are both evident and obscure grounds for all their differences. At this level, they go deeper and become conscious of themselves and their hidden motives. Then, genuine transformation begins when they realize that their conflicts are actually the same conflicts that their parents faced. The truth dawns on them that they are actually adapting their parents' tendencies and behavioural patterns; that in fact, the influence of their parents lives in them and that the actual disagreement is between the wife's mother and the husband's father.

The husband and wife can now see that they are imitating their parents in the way they handle conflicts. The wife perceives that she reacts the same way as her mother when she is upset while the husband realizes that he is like his father when handling conflicts with his wife. This discovery leads them to begin the process of self-inquiry. A woman may not only possess the traits and tendencies of her mother, but that of her father's as well. The same is true with the man. Sometimes, the behaviour can also be a response pattern to counter the parent's behaviour. If the father is a miser and the daughter never got anything from him, she may become very possessive with things. She may, for example, tend to pick a fight with her husband when he gives gifts to other people.

At the fourth level, they begin to think honestly, becoming aware of why they do what they do. The wife examines herself as to why she throws things when she is angry and realizes that her mother used to do the same thing. The husband also probes the reason why he goes away to some place to be alone when he gets angry and realizes that his father also did the same thing. Ironically, couples who have seen their parents fighting and arguing often say to themselves that when they grow up they would never do the same to their spouses. But constant exposure to their parents has subconsciously made them imbibe the same behavioural patterns. These insights create a desire in the couple to break away from the tendencies and patterns of their parents, bringing them to a higher level in their relationship.

Fifth Level

At this level, they perceive that their approach to handling conflicts does not just stem from the behavioural patterns they have inherited from their parents, but is mainly influenced by the beliefs and value system that they have assimilated from their parents and from society in general. For example, there are certain notions that we have adopted regarding male and female roles and responsibilities. In India (and some countries) for instance, it is generally considered improper for men to wash utensils because it is a woman's job, while women are not supposed to clean cars because it is a man's job. Our actions are often guided by certain persuasions as to how males and females should conduct themselves in society. At this level, the husband and wife realize their gender biases and decide to set aside old beliefs in favour of new ways of thinking. They now live and operate out of freedom, peace, love, and happiness. This freedom from within is real independence. After confronting the real issues and underlying beliefs, they find the right remedy for solving conflicts. Two drops of the right medicine (of understanding) start to bring in the results that they want, instead of ten drops of the wrong one. The couple now enjoys the power in the relationship, sharing the same viewpoint and level of consciousness. For it is the discrepancy between the individual levels of consciousness between couples that brings about dysfunctional families.

Sixth Level

The sixth level is characterized by the end of disputes and what remains is not just love, but "bright" love. Bright love is supreme love which is beyond love and hatred. Transactional love and reason-seeking love end, and what develops is unconditional love. At this level, the relationship is not dependent on give and take: "You do this for me. I'll do that for you. If you don't, then I won't…" All conditions cease because love is complete in itself. The couple enjoys freedom and bliss, and their source of happiness is bright love which is the only way to happiness. Here they have the understanding that "love is not what you get but what you give." The focus is only on giving unconditionally and if the other person gives something in return, it is a bonus. But they do not get trapped in the bonuses. The sixth level usually emerges from an elevation in the spiritual understanding of both.

Seventh Level

On the seventh level, there is full expression of unconditional love—where bright love reaches its destination. The highest form of unconditional love now manifests itself and becomes what we call "devotion." It is the supreme state of love akin to what Meerabai had for the Lord which she demonstrated throughout her life. This type of rare devotional love exists between a devotee and God or between a disciple and the Guru.

How to Move to Higher Levels?

To conclude, let us also understand that families do not operate from any one level. They tend to be clustered around two or three levels. Most relationships operate from the lower three levels. True joy in relationships can be derived if you move beyond the first three levels.

To move to the higher levels, simply do two things: Contemplate and communicate. Contemplate on questions such as: From which level are you operating? What kind of relationships are you building? What are you creating in the now, around you, in the space of a relationship? Contemplate and elevate your level of relationship and, having contemplated, simply keep communicating and giving feedback to each other.

ACCEPTING — THE CORNERSTONE OF RELATIONSHIPS

In life, we come across many unwanted situations and people that make us unhappy. There is a small but very powerful mantra which can change your social life dramatically and bestow you with peace and happiness. The mantra is:

'Can I accept this?'

The word "this" in the question refers to the things that are affecting you from outside or from within you. For instance, when you are faced with an unfavourable incident or when you have to deal with some unwanted person, just ask yourself, "Can I accept this?" ("This" signifies the unfavourable incident or the unwanted person). Consequently, when you are able to answer "yes" to the question, your power to deal with the difficult situation or person is increased enormously. Saying this mantra allows you to open up yourself to an easier and more gratifying social life.

This little mantra can work wonders. As we learn to accept the difficulties that confront us, we will find that our answer to this question will be 100 percent "yes" when faced with smaller problems and 99 percent "yes" in case of medium problems. As an example, if an insult is thrown at you, your immediate reaction would be to flinch. Or if your neighbour plays blaring music, or perhaps someone has done mischief in your home, then your normal response would be anger. But if, at that moment, you ask yourself, "Can I accept this?" and your answer is "yes," you will immediately be freed of agitating thoughts and a feeling of relief will instantly flow through you. By making it a habit to ask yourself this question in every situation, you will be spared from the stress as well as from an instant aggressive reaction that can spoil your relationships. Later, when you have cooled down, you can communicate your problem to the concerned person much better and more effectively.

On the other hand, if your answer is, "No, I cannot accept this," then you should accept your non-acceptance as well. For example, if you feel, 'I can't tolerate to see this man,' then ask yourself, "Can I accept my unacceptability?" When you accept your unacceptability, something new is created. If you say to yourself, "Okay, this is the way I am. I have faults, but this is fine, I accept it," you will be amazed by the results of this acceptance. A person who is fat or short may be unable to accept himself, or someone may tell himself, "I have ugly teeth and I cannot accept this." But with this mantra, he will say, "Alright, I can accept this non-acceptance." Once you start accepting yourself and your faults, you will be at ease with yourself and it will be easier for you to accept others and their faults as well.

There is another aspect of the technique you can use when your answer to the mantra is negative in some situations. When your answer is "No", give yourself some time, after which, you should ask yourself again. For instance, somebody does something to you and you feel it is not acceptable, so you answer "no" to the question. Just give yourself some time, then ask again, "Can I accept this now?" You will find that a positive answer is likely to emerge in some instances. If the answer is negative yet again, repeat the same question after some more time. A positive answer may not come immediately, but after a while, you will find yourself saying "yes" and this will instantly make you will feel better.

It is important to understand the power of this mantra. Otherwise, this question may arise: "If I am supposed to accept everything, then shouldn't I try to improve my situation? My child is not studying, my boss is not promoting me, my health is not improving. Shouldn't I try to improve these circumstances?" Yes, you should definitely do so, but only after you have fully opened yourself to embrace the situation. If you cannot accept something, how can you work? How can you handle your problems? It is like tying one hand to your back and trying to solve the problem with only one free hand. This is a folly. Common sense tells you that whenever a problem arises, both your hands should be free to be able to solve the problem more easily. Yes, you should definitely try to improve the situation, but you should first learn to accept it. Now, after accepting the situation, you will be surprised how the encounter becomes more powerful and the problem becomes much simpler for you to solve. If you do not take the first step right, all the succeeding steps could go wrong. That is why you have to first learn the art of acceptance and then work towards improving the situation.

Life, just like a river, has boundaries. A life so bounded by unacceptance creates a river of sorrows. However, there is so much space within us to embrace acceptance of the acceptable and especially of the unacceptable. We can accept not just our own sorrows but also the sufferings of the whole world. So if we remove the boundaries, everything flows freely and passes by. If only we do not resist, then the incidents, the misery, and the negative thoughts will melt away and the suffering in our life and consequently in the entire world will disappear.

THE GOLDEN RULE

The Golden Rule mentioned in all religions is: "Do unto others as you would want others to do unto you." It is the primary message of almost every religion and every great master.

Learn to forgive others as well as yourself. When you forgive others, you are not doing a favour to them, but to yourself. Thus, you must learn to forgive.

The Golden Rule is best interpreted as: "Treat others only in ways that you are willing to be treated in exactly the same situation." This means putting yourself in the shoes of the person on the receiving end of your action. If you act in a certain way towards another and yet are unwilling to be treated the same way under the same circumstances, then you violate the rule.

The first step to take in applying the Golden Rule is to simply understand other people's point of view. The next time you have a conversation, instead of jumping ahead with what you plan to say, whether written or verbal, stop and consider what it might be like to be in the other person's shoes. If appropriate, you may choose to spend some time gaining understanding about him by asking questions and listening—truly listening—to his responses. Consider his perspective and how he may feel about things. The more you practise stepping into other people's shoes, the more you will experience its benefits, including the power to communicate meaningfully. In applying this step, simply ask yourself: "If someone were to treat me the way I plan to treat this person, will I be happy about it?"

What we have just discussed is what many have said and understood about the Golden Rule. However, the Golden Rule as taught in the Tej Gyan Foundation (TGF) is on a totally different plane with a totally different perspective. TGF considers this as the Golden Rule: Do unto others as you would want others to do unto you—the one you are in essence beyond the body and mind. Understanding the meaning of who you really are is covered in the next part of this book. You are the Self, the Universal "I." Ponder this: if you want others to treat you as the Self, then what behaviour is expected of you? You will understand the TGF version of the Golden Rule only when you have understood Part 7 of this book. Also, ponder over the Golden Rule as understood by all religions, for this alone is enough to bring social transformation.

GOLDEN RULE

BUDDHISM

Treat not others in ways that you yourself would find hurtful.
The Buddha

HINDUISM

This is the sum of duty: Do not do to others what would cause pain if done to you.
Mahabharata

SIKHISM

I am a stranger to no one: and no one is stranger to me. Indeed I am a friend to all.
Guru Granth Saheb

ISLAM

Not one of you truly believes until you wish for others what you wish for yourself.
The Prophet Mohammad

JAINISM

One should treat all creatures in the world as one would like to be treated.
Mahavir Sutrakritanga

CHRISTIANITY

In everything, do to others as you would have them do to you; for this is the law and the prophets.
Jesus, Mathew

TGF

Do unto others, as you want others to do unto who you are in essence.
Tejguru Sirshree

Social Transformation Action Plan

(1) _____

(2) _____

(3) _____

(4) _____

(5) _____

(6) _____

(7) _____

(8) _____

(9) _____

(10) _____

(11) _____

(12) _____

(13) _____

(14) _____

(15) _____

(16) _____

(17) _____

(18) _____

(19) _____

(20) _____

Part 7

Spiritual Transformation: Encounter with the Self

THE AIM OF SPIRITUALITY IS HAPPINESS

Everyone desires happiness. But happiness is temporary. The quest of spirituality is the quest for permanent happiness, the quest for true happiness—a kind of bliss that does not diminish with time. Man in his day-to-day life seeks this permanent happiness, but in the process gets entangled in illusory happiness or false happiness.

But what is this illusory or false happiness?

… it is seeking happiness in praise.

… it is what you derive out of winning a lottery.

… it is what you derive when you get a promotion.

… it is found in taunting or even harming others.

… it is found in indulging the palate.

Transforming the way you derive happiness is the first step to spiritual transformation. There are seven levels of happiness. All the examples of false happiness discussed above are categorized under the lower levels of happiness. As you transform spiritually, you derive happiness from the higher levels.

Level 1 Happiness: Artificial Happiness

The first level of happiness is a kind of happiness that does not actually exist because it is derived from doing an unlawful or improper act. For example, it gives you pleasure to get away with riding the bus and arriving at your destination without paying for the bus ticket. There is actually no sense in feeling happy about what you did, and yet it tickles you. It is just a mirage.

Level 2 Happiness: Second-Hand Happiness

Second-hand happiness is derived from using others for your own pleasure—for example, by being sadistic, or teasing, taunting, or harming others just for the fun of it. It is like finding happiness in using a second-hand car, i.e. a car that was previously owned by someone else. Second-hand objects do not last long, nor does second-hand happiness.

Level 3 Happiness: Stimulation Happiness

Stimulation happiness refers to happiness that is gained from the excitement brought about by partying or entertainment. For instance, you find thrill and excitement in attending parties and celebrations, in watching a television program or a favourite sport, or even engaging in gambling. This is stimulation happiness. We live in a society that caters to people's desire to be entertained. While it stimulates delight, the stimulation does not last long. Two or three days after the excitement of a party or game, one may feel bored and unfulfilled, and therefore begin to seek a higher level of excitement. This may lead one to turn to gambling or some other form of addiction.

Level 4 Happiness: Formula Happiness

Many people have created a formula for happiness and seeing the formula working for them gives them much satisfaction. The formula may be as simple as "reading a Sunday morning newspaper + having tea or coffee + smoking a cigarette." Or it may be "a Saturday night party + a new date." For children, the formula could be "a whole day of play + pizzas or burgers + a movie to end the day" or "Sunday + a visit to the amusement park." For ladies, it could be "Flowers + Gift (preferably diamonds or gold) = Happiness."

Level 5 Happiness: Happiness in Service

This is considered the first among the higher levels of happiness, where an individual derives happiness out of serving others. The law of nature says: "Whatever you become a medium for, it will multiply in your life." According to this law, the more one serves, the more nature rewards him, and therefore the happier one becomes and finds joy in this virtuous cycle. However, many a time, this also leads to bloated egos and high expectations from others. It does not take long, therefore, when the person falls into the depths of unhappiness after reaching the heights of happiness derived at this level.

Level 6 Happiness: Divine Happiness

At this level, man is in love with the Creator. He sings the praises of God and admires everything created by God. He completely embraces everything that happens in his life and says: "If it is God's desire to keep me in this state, then I am happy. If God wants me to cry, then I will cry with happiness in my heart." It is a very beautiful state born out of surrender. There is a level of understanding and spiritual growth from which this happiness emanates. One always feels gratitude and devotion at this level.

Level 7 Happiness: Eternal Bliss

Each one of us bears the eternal bliss within, but we are not aware of it. When you are in deep sleep and your mind is neither awake, nor dreaming, nor aware of the body, then you are in connection with that eternal state. Before the mind of a child fully develops, he is established in the same state of eternal bliss. But then, as the child grows, everyone starts conditioning his mind to make him believe that he is an individual, a body. Eventually, identification with the body is complete, and here begins unhappiness. When the child is fully grown, he starts to think that happiness can be derived only from the lower levels described earlier. However, if self-realization occurs through the grace of a Guru or God, then there is access to the state of eternal bliss. This is permanent happiness which does not diminish with the passing of time. Actually, the more you access it, the more the happiness grows.

Regain the eternal bliss that all children experience and become like a child (not childish). For this transformation to occur, you have to learn to open up and blossom.

42

OPEN UP AND BLOSSOM IN LIFE

There are three kinds of people in this world: those who become closed to all situations, those who are stuck with every situation, and those who are open. All of them need to understand a very simple secret—that life is all about blossoming. To move to higher levels of happiness, one must open up and blossom in life.

The closed ones are those who withdraw and fold up whenever an opportunity or a situation presents itself. They withdraw when faced with unpleasant circumstances, like when they are laughed at, or when confronted with difficult people. They snivel, shudder, and shrink, resisting every problem they encounter, whether big or small. But when they realize (if they realize at all) the secret of life—that it is all about blossoming—then life becomes magical to them and this realization makes them wonder how they could have survived for so long in that closed state. They realize that their lives have become filled with fear and worry, having been bereft of this simple secret. Thus, for the closed, understanding the secret of blossoming is an amazing and magical experience.

Then, there are those who are stuck some way or the other. They are entangled and trapped in their own small worlds, always feeling suppressed. Although they are better than the closed as they do not withdraw further, but they get caught in one place, and stop growing or expanding. Many opportunities come their way, but they are so stuck with their little problems and way of living, that it is of no avail. While they may have surmounted big challenges, they fail to move forward because of something extremely insignificant. Some are stuck with the idea of revenge, some with the misconception that they have been wronged, and this makes them seethe with hatred. When these kinds of people realize the secret that life is all about blossoming, they are released and so is their energy. It is like being able to clean themselves from all the filth within him as well as the filth that they have accumulated from constantly observing it in others. Their web of illusions and myths about life are instantly cleared.

Then, there are those who are open—open to growth and neither withdrawing nor remaining stuck in one place. Just a little push and they start to blossom. For them, realizing the secret of life is like taking off in a helicopter. To illustrate, when you are driving around the city, roads can get pretty confusing and you may end up getting lost. But once you view the roads from the top riding a helicopter, the whole picture is revealed and the direction becomes clear. This is the case with those who realize and imbibe the secret of blossoming. They take off with utmost clarity and foresight.

What is this secret of blossoming all about? It is quite simple and all it says is that every circumstance in life appears only to give you an opportunity to blossom. Every incident occurs to test you and to see if you blossom or not. Look at children and animals. Do they withdraw at every opportunity? They live naturally and operate out of their being. They operate from nothingness and are totally open. They intuitively know this secret of life. But as people grow up, they begin to withdraw and start closing up. A time comes when they completely withdraw into a shell and their hearts become cold and closed to life's opportunities. But the earlier they realize the secret, the better it is for them to be able to return to a childlike way of living and looking at life.

Let us do a small exercise to understand what blossoming is all about. While reading this book, check your posture. If you feel stressed, change your posture and relax. Raise up your arms towards the sky and open your hands fully. Tell yourself that you are open to receive all the blessings and blossoming that life has to offer. Feel the happiness, the pleasure of blooming. Be in this posture for 30 seconds. Now, put your hands down.

Did you feel more relaxed? Did you feel open? Practise this during times of stress. In life, we do not get many chances to blossom and open up. We neither talk openly nor walk openly. The real journey can begin when we start opening up.

Understand the secret of blossoming and opening up so that you can experience bliss every moment of your life.

THE QUALITY OF YOUR LIFE IS GOVERNED BY THE QUALITY OF YOUR QUESTIONS

In order to achieve spiritual transformation, as you ascend to higher levels of happiness the quality of the questions you ask needs to change. Your questions are a reflection of your thoughts, feelings, understanding, and outlook. There are five levels of questioning, and for true transformation to occur, your questions should be of the higher levels.

Level 1 Questions: Questions for the Sake of Questioning

At the first level, an individual asks questions merely for the sake of questioning. He is not actually interested in knowing the answers.

Level 2 Questions: Questions for Passing Time

These are questions asked with an intention to listen to the answer, but not to learn. The question is posed just because somebody is available to answer the question and there is pretty much nothing else to do. These questions could also take the shape of sarcastic or taunting questions.

Level 3 Questions: Questions for Utilizing Time

These are higher level questions asked with an intention to learn and use time constructively. You come across someone very knowledgeable, so you ask questions and really learn from the answers. These are not aimless queries, but are questions that make the best use of time.

Level 4 Questions: Incisive Questions

These are in-depth questions on a given topic, and are not usually asked by anybody and everybody. Before asking such questions, a person should have done a thorough study of the subject. Incisive questions do not arise without reflection. Those who ask such questions never stop growing.

Level 5 Questions: Seeker's Questions

These are not questions on just any topic. These are the most profound questions of all such as: Who am I? Why am I here? What is eternal joy? What is life? A seeker does not ask them out of curiosity or eagerness, but out of his intense thirst to know the answers to these questions. It is a matter of life and death to him.

Level 5 questions are those that elevate your level of consciousness. How many level 5 questions do you ask yourself or others through the day? The more focused you are on Level 5 questions, the faster your complete transformation will be. If you have level 5 questions, you can send them to Tej Gyan Foundation and you shall receive the answers to them.

44

SHATTER THE FRAMEWORK OF YOUR WORLD

As you progress towards higher levels of happiness through higher level questions, remember that "life" has been given to you for one purpose only. Every incident in life can take you forward or backward. We have already seen in Part 1 how self transformation is all about converting snakes into ladders. The best way to do this is to use every incident of life to break out of the framework with which you perceive the world.

Every moment of every day, various incidents take place around you which either make you feel good or bad. Each of us desires to have good feelings within us, but the question is: how can we feel good about each day and each incident?

After any incident, whether you are feeling good or bad, ask yourself: Was the feeling an experience of my own body or someone else's? If, presumably, it was yours, then who can be held responsible for it? If that feeling is to be changed, who should make the change? Will it be someone else or yourself? When you contemplate on these questions, you gain the insight that:

(1) Your get the feeling of every experience within your body.

(2) You are responsible for that feeling, not your neighbour or the world.

(3) If you want the bad feelings to change, then nobody else can do it for you.

(4) Having understood this, how then are you feeling at the moment? Are you feeling as you want to, or is it something else?

(5) If you are feeling bad, then are you prepared to change it?

(6) If yes, then when will you change it?

Here and Now

It does not take much to change feelings, and if you so desire, you can immediately change them. Doing so can change the framework of your world. Every individual has a different outlook and a different framework, which determine his actions. If you hold someone else responsible for your sorrows, then you can never be happy. You need to take responsibility of your sorrow and your happiness as well.

From now on, with every incident, ask yourself these questions: "If I am feeling miserable or sad, who is responsible for my feelings? Who can change it? When can I change it?" When you have answered these questions honestly, you will find yourself feeling happy... and you yourself will be responsible for it.

45

THE WHOLE SOLE PURPOSE OF YOUR LIFE

We have within us a centre, a core. You can call that centre the source of thoughts and feelings. This centre is always stable. It is akin to a clock which has hands that move, but the spindle always remains stationary. Similarly, for a fan to move round and round, a stationary central rod is needed. Like these objects, there is something within us which is stationary or fixed. The sole purpose of life is to be established in that centre. Once you have access to that centre, you will learn that there alone lies eternal bliss. As the level of your questions rises, you will see all answers directly or indirectly pointing to that centre—the bright centre (tejasthan). That centre can also be called the Self. Being established there permanently is what is also called Self-Stabilization, which is distinct from Self-Realization. Self-Realization is only a one-time glimpse.

There are three steps needed to attain the sole purpose of life.

Step 1: Be Positive-Minded

Always have a positive outlook while heading towards your sole purpose. You might encounter negative thoughts in your journey.

Accordingly, you must convert every negative thought into a positive one by using the word "but." If you start thinking to yourself, "I am feeling sad," then you should instead say, "I am sad, but if I desire, I can experience the feeling of bliss here and now." If you think, "I cannot do this work," then reframe the thought in this manner: "I cannot do this, but with the help of God it is possible."

Step 2: Be Present-Minded

At this step, you are required to keep yourself alert with every sound, every incident, and every thought. By doing so, you will become sensitive about yourself and your surroundings. You will also get rid of forgetfulness and will no longer remain absent-minded. Your awareness of the present will also make you aware of your defilements or negative emotions such as hatred, disgust, anger, pride, envy, greed, lust, etc. Thus, your mind starts to become pure. Practise living in the present using all the methods and meditations described in Part 4 of this book.

Step 3: Be Single-Minded

At the third step, you are focused only towards the sole purpose of your life. Remind yourself of this purpose throughout the day. It is the law of life that whatever you are receptive towards or whatever is the focus of your attention becomes manifest in your life. Be single-minded to get stabilized in your centre, so that you can experience total liberation and eternal bliss.

These three steps take your mind within. The mind is the cloud that is shrouding the sun (Self) from shining. When your mind surrenders to the centre, then the eternal happiness, the love, and the silence (moun) become manifest; and what is always present can now be experienced. Practice Self Inquiry which can give you additional help to reach the Self, to reach the centre. Self Inquiry is also one of the best methods to take your mind within so that it gets eliminated and the Self shines through.

46

SELF ENQUIRY

What is Self Inquiry?

The technique of Self Inquiry is one of raising doubt over the mind, questioning the mind itself—the very mind that raises doubts over the whole world and asks: Who made this world? Where will I go when I die? Why was I born? What is the purpose of life?, and so on. But, who is asking all these questions? When we ask this, the mind starts falling for the first time. Let us say that the mind is asking: "What will happen when I die?" At that moment, if you ask, "Who will die?", then the mind is forced to go within. Within lies absolute silence, and in that silence the death of the mind occurs momentarily. Going within, you discover for the first time that there is nothing that can be called the mind! To train the mind to perform Self Inquiry, first practise "inquiry of the body-mind."

Inquiry of the Body-Mind

Inquire about your body-mind with honesty. Then Self Inquiry will become simple. In this kind of inquiry you start observing the mind in its different facets, states, and relationships. You will see how the mind changes from moment to moment and how it puts on various masks. Do not hide the truth from yourself, instead report to yourself honestly. You may not like to see your own mind's darker aspects, but transformation will not occur without doing so. If you start observing yourself in every situation, then very soon you will be transformed, and for the first time you will begin to understand the mind.

Every night, before retiring, look back at the entire day that has just passed, or at least recall the major events. You will then see for yourself the "nature" of your body-mind mechanism. Ask yourself: "In all the different situations I faced, what were my actions and what was my motive for such actions?" For example, if you did not do the work that was assigned to you, why did you not do so? Was it because the person who assigned you the work does not boost your ego? Or was it because he is a thorn to your ambitions and aspirations? But if you did the work that you were asked to do, why did you do it? Was it because you were afraid of that person? Or was it because that person boosts your ego? Do not hide from yourself but rather give yourself honest answers. If you like somebody, what is the reason? Is it because of the things he does for you or is it his qualities? If you do not like somebody, is it because you find him obnoxious or is it because he poses as an obstacle to your preferred ways of handling things? Answer in all sincerity.

To make the inquiry even more rigorous, reflect on your actions every hour of the day and ask yourself the motive of your actions for that hour. Check which of the following 12 states of mind you were in during the past hour.

A	Anger:	Feeling of rage on yourself or on others
B	Boredom:	Not being interested in anything
C	Confusion:	Not understanding in spite of explanations

D	Depression:	Feeling of melancholy with or without reason
E	Ego:	It is I, me, myself; taking credit; self-praise
F	Fear:	Feeling afraid; feeling uncertain
G	Guilt:	Self-criticism (Why did I do that?)
H	Happiness:	State of bliss
I	Ill-will/Hatred:	Wanting to hurt somebody
J	Jealousy:	"Why don't I have that which the other person has?"
K	Kindness:	Wanting to benefit others and making others happy
L	Laziness:	Not wanting to do anything; being idle

Ask yourself a question every hour of the day: "Right now, how is the state of my mind?" Check yourself on the 12 points from A to L. You will find that the desires of the mind and the states of the mind keep changing. Instability or constant change is its nature. At various times you will see that the mind is anxious, happy, angry, full of greed, scared, withdrawn, worried, or depressed. At other times, it is full of hatred for somebody and sometimes full of guilt. Still at times, it is egoistic or deceitful or honest or logical. Then again, at other times, it is comparing or imaginative, and absent-minded or fully aware. This inquiry every hour will yield miraculous results. Soon after, you will know your mind completely. By experience, and not by mere intellect, you will know that the mind is just like a monkey that keeps on jumping from place to place. It cannot stay put in any one state. If the mind is indeed so, then why do we get attached to it? This knowledge will dawn upon you. "If the mind is disturbed, then it is not me who is disturbed." Such clarity will arise and this experience will influence your daily life. Thoughts of happiness or unhappiness will not be able to dislodge you from your centre. It is the mind that is either anxious or relaxed. You will get the insight that "anger, hatred, guilt, fear—these are all with the mind, not with me." You will also realize that "this moment-by-moment change in the mind does not affect my bright happiness in any way at all." Then, you will be peaceful (from within) even during stress. Your understanding will be: "Stress is with the body and mind, not with me. This stress has occurred to get something specific done from my body."

You will know all the ups and downs of your body-mind mechanism through your own experience and thus you can proceed towards Self Inquiry, which is the second and last step. The first step is the inquiry of the body-mind mechanism; the second is that of Self Inquiry. In the first step, one carries out the inquiry of the body-mind mechanism and sees all its possible behaviours. In the second step, one has to know the one who owns the mechanism. Who is he? Who am I? Who was born? Who will die? Who sleeps? Who awakens? Who walks? Who sits? Due to whose being does this entire universe function? Who? Who?

Self Inquiry

Having practised inquiry of the body-mind mechanism, Self Inquiry is the next logical step. Now the mind is already trained to look at itself. In Self Inquiry, you leave behind all other questions and focus on only one—Who am I? This is one such thought which will eliminate every other thought, notion, belief, and concept. All we need to learn is how to use this potent weapon.

The method of practising Self Inquiry is as follows: Whenever a thought arises—of fear, greed, rejection, worry, etc.—ask yourself: "To whom has this thought occurred?" or "Who was afraid?" or "Who felt the rejection?" and so forth. The reply will be, "To me." Then ask, "Who is this me? Who am I?" You will reach your centre (source) whenever this question arises, and for some time you will be immersed in the supreme silence (moun). In this silence will arise the Supreme Truth. Another thought will appear after a few moments. You will again ask the question, "To whom has this thought occurred?" This question will cut the thought short and the reply will be "To me." Then ask again, "Who am I?"

You may begin with 20 minutes of Self Inquiry every day, and very soon you will be able to continue this inquiry through the course of the day even while working and also know the reply through your own experience. In this way, the thought "Who am I?" will wipe out all other thoughts and will finally wipe out itself.

Whenever any other thought arises, ask yourself, "To whom has this thought occurred?" (Who is the thinker?). It does not matter how many thoughts come to you. When you ask this to yourself, the answer may be, "This thought has occurred to me." Immediately ask yourself, "Who is this me? Who am I?" You will be thrown back to yourself. When you ask yourself these questions, do not give the answer in words. Do not answer from the intellect, saying such things as "I am Consciousness" or "I am Self." Beyond these answers, beyond the intellect, you have to experience the feeling of your being—the feeling of sense of presence. Reaching the experience of the true self is the real answer to this question. In this way, every thought will take you back to your true self every time. Right now, if you are thinking, "I cannot understand this," then ask, "Who is the one that cannot understand? If I have not understood, then who am I . . . who . . . who?" Immediately you will see that thoughts disappear for a few moments and you become thoughtless. Only the Self remains. In this way, by repeatedly going onto your true self, the mind will weaken and the light of consciousness will begin to shine through. With repeated practice, the mind will learn to stay at its source. By dipping into the Self again and again, the mind will dissolve. It is like the story of the dolls made out of salt.

They wanted to dive into the sea to measure its depth, but slowly they themselves dissolved.

Perform this Self Inquiry until you find out your true identity, until your concepts about yourself dissolve—the root concept being that you are the body. The moment these concepts or beliefs dissolve, Self Inquiry will end because now you would have stabilized on yourself. You would have attained higher states of the Self. As you proceed to higher states of the Self, even if there are thoughts, you would have understood that they are not yours. "They do not come to me. I am the supreme witness beyond them. Thoughts are in my body-mind mechanism. This machine is just a mirror, which makes me aware of myself. If there are thoughts arising in this mirror, how can they trouble me? The main thing is that this mirror always does its work—it always reveals my presence to me." (That means it always makes me aware of my awareness.) Practising Self Inquiry, and thus being established in oneself, is the highest devotion of all. Eliminating thoughts the moment they arise through the process of Self Inquiry is the greatest and truest sacrifice of all.

Self Inquiry is elucidated in more detail in the book Self Inquiry with Understanding published by Tej Gyan Foundation. As you read the book and practise Self Inquiry, you start ascending the higher steps of consciousness and thus begin to attain higher states of Self.

SPIRITUAL TRANSFORMATION AND BEYOND . . . 12 STEPS AND 12 STATES

The road to spiritual transformation is a 12-step path and there are 12 states that are progressively experienced.

The 12 Steps

The mind of the seeker can either aid or abort his spiritual progress. There are 12 steps that a seeker progresses through. The mind can get stuck at any of these steps. The mind ought to be given the understanding that it has to keep progressing up the steps if the seeker wants to achieve complete spiritual transformation.

Step 1: What?

As a child grows, he starts asking "what" questions. He wants to explore everything and asks: "What is this? What is that?" The first step then is the question that the child poses to the world: "What?"

Step 2: How?

As the child begins to learn new words and the words begin to make some sense to him, the question "what" slowly starts to lose its significance. The second step unfolds and the child begins to ask "how" questions. He asks everyone: "How does this work? How does that work?" Children nowadays know the answer to the question "how" fairly early. They can operate computers, mobile phones, and other gadgets at a very early age.

Step 3: Why?

The third step is a critical juncture. The child starts asking "why" questions. Parents find themselves in a fix when the child asks, "Why did that person die?" Parents can at the most explain that he died due to sickness. The child then asks, "But why do people die at all?" Parents are often at a loss for words with these kinds of questions, so they tell the child not to ask "why" for everything. The child then asks, "Why shouldn't I?"

Step 4: I Know

When the question "why" is suppressed, many children erroneously form their own conclusions and stop at Step 4. They have got a few ready-made answers from their elders to the question "why." They have received some basic kindergarten answers to the most profound questions of life. With this, the child, now a youth, starts to imagine that he knows it all.

Step 5: I Don't Know

At this step, the youth listens to a discourse or maybe reads a book; and then it hits him that he does not know much. Many do not progress to this step. The youth is very fortunate to have received the first gem of wisdom—that he does not know everything; that he is not wise at all.

Step 6: I Am in KG

The youth, then, starts understanding various concepts of spirituality such as karma, heaven and hell, liberation, etc. He assimilates all the answers, but there is still a vacuum inside him. He wants to know more and wants the final answers. He realizes that all he knows is either general knowledge (GK), or mere knowledge of kindergarten (KG) spirituality. But now, he is a bit wiser. The answers he has received are not wrong. They have their own place, but they are correct at the level of kindergarten spirituality only. The thirst for the final answers begins to arise.

Step 7: I Want to Know

At this step, he has become a seeker. Now the thirst to know the final answers becomes more intense. He yearns to know the truth. A thought emerges within him that he wants to be liberated from all other thoughts. This is a happy thought. He has now progressed through steps, from saying "I don't know" or "I may not know" to the stage of saying "I must know."

Step 8: I have Knowledge

At this step, he understands the truth "intellectually." He knows the meaning of duality, non-duality, Self at Rest, Self in Action, etc. at the intellectual level. At this transformational step, he derives happiness from intellectually knowing and understanding "the truth."

Step 9: I am Knowledge

At this step, the seeker understands that what he is, is nothing but knowledge itself. Now he has progressed from intellectually knowing and saying that "I have knowledge" to experiencing that "I am Knowledge." He understands that there is no one "else" to know the knowledge. There is no separate individual that will be left at the end of the process to know the knowledge. Only Knowledge actually exists. Only the Experience of the Self actually exists. The Experience is experiencing the Experience through Experience in Experience. At this step in the transformation of the seeker, the seeker and the sought are no longer separate. The seeker and the knowledge sought are no longer distinct.

Step 10: "I am" is Knowledge

At Step 10, he transcends further. Now even the thought that "I am Knowledge" is transcended and only "I am" remains. This is the Bright Wisdom (The wisdom beyond knowledge and ignorance—Tejgyan) that arises. However "I" continues to exist. With the experience of "I am," the knowledge is complete.

Step 11: "Am" is

At Step 11, the "I" also ceases to exist and so does the knowledge. What remains is just "am," "am-ness," "is-ness." "Beingness" in the truest sense begins… just being… just presence.

Step 12: Bright Silence

At this step, there are no words, just Bright Silence. Bright Silence is the silence beyond sound and silence. It is the original state of the Self in which words emerge and then fall back to fade away. It is always there in the background. After Step 12, the expression or demonstration of the bright silence, (or the Self), begins. Only after all 12 steps have been ascended does "life" in its truest sense begin.

The 12 States

In every man's life, there are various states of being that occur—the state of being happy, the state of being sad, the state of being alive, the state of being dead, and so on. All these states can be classified under two main states:

State 1

The State of the Body-Mind (external state)

State 2

The State of the Self (internal state)

Every enlightened master has described the state of the Self which is an internal state of bliss, silence, and devotion. People hear what they describe and then prescribe the same to themselves. They try to become silent and close their eyes but do not experience that internal state because they are still on the level of the body-mind, where the body-mind wants to experience the Self. The external state can never experience the internal state. The internal state manifests when the external state is subdued and non-interfering. The internal state of silence, bliss, and devotion always exists. But because man is heavily focused on the external state, he cannot access what is always readily available to him. He then listens to a discourse and tries to reach the internal state through the external state, but that is not possible. The internal state manifests when the mind (the judgmental, comparing mind) becomes empty. The internal state—the Self—is always available to be accessed.

The States of the Self (Internal State)

State 3

Self at Rest (God in Rest)

State 4

Self in Action (God in Expression)

The state of Self at Rest is when the world was not yet created, an unexpressed state when He was alone, when only Shiva existed, where only the subject was, where only the Father was, when the Experience was there but could not experience itself. Out of this state arose the state of Self in Action, the Expression of God, where Shiva created Shakti, where the subject created the object to experience itself, where the Father created the Son.

There are two further states of Self in Action.

The States of Self in Action

State 5

Identified Self (When the Self identifies with the body and considers that to be "I")

State 6

Disidentified Self (Self Realization—disidentification from the body)

When the Self (Experience) is united with the body, it is called Self in Action. The Experience can experience itself only in action. It can witness itself only on creation (expression). In the Self at Rest state, there is no need for experience. That is why seekers at Tej Gyan Foundation are told to become Bright Ignorants. The root state is one of ignorance. When the Self identifies with the body, the journey of knowledge and ignorance begins. From the state of Self at Rest, the world has manifested—a world with many bodies. This is the state of Self in Action. When the Self identifies itself with the body, assuming itself to be the body, the "individual" gets created. This is Self in Action in the identified state, which can be classified into four more states. In a few rare cases, this individual attains Self Realization where the Self gets disidentified with the body while the body is alive.

The States of the Identified Self

State 7

Identified with the body as an individual and being unhappy (entangled)

The Self is identified with the body. It assumes itself to be a separate individual. And is unhappy. (But all of this is a mere game. As far as the Self is concerned, there is nothing like good or bad, happiness or unhappiness.) Now the identified Self is unhappy, and in an unhappy state it gets more and more entangled in the individual and his world. There are many individuals who are unhappy in life and create unhappiness for others. There is little possibility of their coming out of the unhappiness since they are so trapped and entangled. Untangling takes place only in those few individuals who come in contact with a higher state (enlightened soul). Else, the unhappiness and the entangling only become stronger in majority of such bodies.

State 8

Identified with the body as an individual and seeking a way to be liberated from unhappiness (untangling)

This is a state where the Self is unhappy, but is using the unhappiness as a medium to untangle itself. Unhappiness never comes for its own sake but bears a lesson. The Self is learning from it and is trying to return to its original state.

State 9

Identified with the body as an individual and being happy (egoistic and entangled)

In this state, the Self is identified with the body and is happy, but is still entangled. Happiness is being used to boost the ego. The individual in question has everything in life—all the material pleasures. But the materialistic objects are being used to get more entangled in the illusory world of "ego" (separate individual). Consequently, no importance is given by the individual to anyone except oneself. Everyone else is looked down upon.

State 10

Identified with the body as an individual and being happy, but in the process of untangling (transforming)

In this state, the Self is identified with the body and is happy. But here, happiness is not a shackle. All the material things are being used to untangle itself in that body. Money is used to buy the best of facilities for meditation. Power is used to serve the Truth.

States of the Disidentified Self

State 11

Witnessing

In this state, the Self has begun to stabilize on itself. Before achieving this state, let's say you were in a room and you were seeing the fan, the chairs, the walls, etc. in the room. You were asked, "Why are you seeing all this?" You replied that there is nothing else to do but to see. But in this state of witnessing, even when external objects are witnessed, the journey that happens is inward. The inner witnessing is given more importance. This means the Self witnesses itself inside the body as well as outside in the whole of its Creation.

State 12

Expressing

In this state, it is like you are still in the room and seeing the fans, the chairs, and the walls, but you express yourself by coming out of the room. On disidentification with the body, there are only two options left—witnessing or expressing. This is not expression or demonstration of the body. This is the expression of the Self through the body… where now, through this body, other bodies too are being taught the art of untangling.

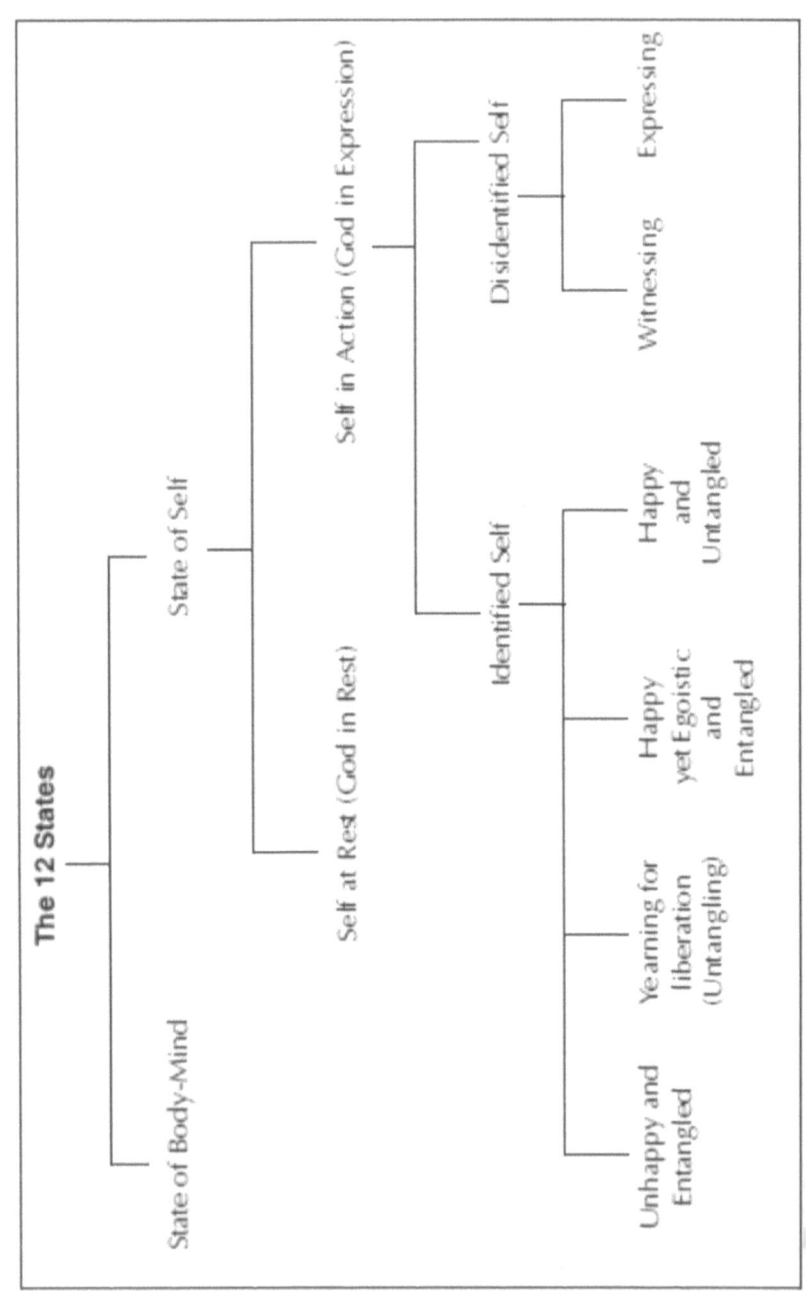

48

SUMMING IT UP . . .
SELF TRANSFORMATION IS THE TRANSFORMATION OF THE SELF

We have understood that when it comes to complete self transformation, there are levels of happiness, and that we have to open up and blossom and ascend these levels of happiness. To do this, there are levels of questions that you need to ask. You need to be single-minded about helping your mind turn inward during any incident and shatter the framework with which you see the world. There are various steps that you must attend to in order to attain the Self and various states of the Self that have to be progressively experienced. So then a logical question arises: Can I attain the Self?

The previous chapter would have made it clear to you that Self Transformation is the transformation of the Self. It does not mean transformation of an individual by himself alone, but with someone who has walked the steps—someone with a higher state to show you the path. The journey is such that, though there are steps and states, there is not really "somewhere" to go to. It is a journey that begins as well as ends at the destination. Hence, the importance of a guide on this journey can never be overemphasized. Thus, Self Transformation is a journey where a Guru or a spiritual master is very much required; not just any guide, but a guide who has walked the path and is very much alive, giving you feedback and guiding your transformation process. That you may find such a Guru is my good wish for you.

You can mail your opinion or feedback on this book to: books.feedback@tejgyan.org

About Sirshree

Sirshree's spiritual quest, which began during his childhood, led him on a journey through various schools of philosophy and meditation practices. He studied a wide range of literature on mind science and spirituality. After a long period of deep contemplation on the truth of life, his quest culminated in attaining the ultimate truth.

Sirshree espouses, "All spiritual paths that lead to the truth begin differently but culminate at the same point – Understanding. This understanding is complete in itself. Listening to this understanding is enough to attain the Truth." Over the last two decades, he has dedicated his life to raise mass consciousness.

Sirshree has delivered more than 4000 discourses that throw light on this understanding. He has designed a system for wisdom, which makes it accessible to all. This system has inspired people from all walks of life to progress on their journey of the Truth. Thousands of seekers join in a virtual prayer for World Peace and Global Healing daily at 9:09 am and 9:09 pm.

About Tej Gyan Foundation

Tej Gyan Foundation is a non-profit organization founded on the teachings of Sirshree. The Foundation disseminates Tejgyan – the wisdom that guides one from self-development to Self-realization, leading towards Self-stabilization.

The Foundation's system for imparting wisdom has been assessed by international quality auditors and accredited with the ISO 9001:2015 certification. This wisdom has been presented in a simple, systematic, and practically applicable form that makes it accessible to people from all walks of life, regardless of religion, caste, social strata, country, or belief system.

The Foundation has centers in more than 400 cities and towns across India and other countries. The mission of Tej Gyan Foundation is to create a highly evolved society by leading seekers from negative thoughts to positive thoughts and further, from positive thoughts to Happy thoughts. A 'Happy thought' is the auspicious thought of being free from all thoughts, leading to the state of supreme bliss beyond thoughts.

If you seek such wisdom that leads you beyond mere knowledge, dissolves all problems, frees you from all limiting beliefs, reveals the true nature of divinity, and establishes you in the ultimate truth, then it is time to discover Tejgyan; it is time to rise above the mundane knowledge of words and experience Tejgyan!

The MahaAasmani Magic of Awakening Retreat

Self-development to Self-realization towards Self-stabilization

Do you wish to experience unconditional happiness that is not dependent on any reason? Happiness that is permanent and only increases with time? Do you wish to experience love, peace, self-belief, harmony in relationships, prosperity, and true contentment? Do you wish to progress in all facets of your life, viz. physical, mental, social, financial, and spiritual?

If you seek answers to these questions and are thirsty for the ultimate truth, then you are welcome to participate in the MahaAasmani Magic of Awakening retreat organized by Tej Gyan Foundation. This is the Foundation's flagship retreat based on the teachings of Sirshree.

The purpose of this retreat

The purpose of this retreat is that every human being should:

- Discover the answer to "Who am I" and "Why am I?" through direct experience and be established in ultimate bliss.

- Learn the art of living in the present, free from the burden of the past and the anxiety of the future.

- Acquire practical tools to help quieten the chattering mind and dissolve problems.

- Discover missing links in the practices of Meditation (*Dhyana*), Action (*Karma*), Wisdom (*Gyana*), and Devotion (*Bhakti*).

About Books by Sirshree

Sirshree's published work includes more than 150 book titles, some of which have been translated into more than 10 languages. His literature provides a profound reading on various topics of practical living and unravels the missing links in karma, wisdom, devotion, meditation, and consciousness.

His books have been published by leading publishing houses like Penguin, Hay House, Bloomsbury, Wisdom Tree, Jaico, etc. "The Source" book series, authored by Sirshree, has sold over 10 million copies. Various luminaries and celebrities like His Holiness the Dalai Lama, publishers Mr. Reid Tracy, Ms. Tami Simon and Yoga Master Dr. B. K. S. Iyengar have released Sirshree's books and lauded his work.

The Source
Attain Both, Inner Peace
and Worldly success

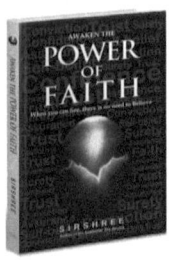

Awaken the Power of Faith
Discover the 7 Principles of the
Highest Power of the Universe

To order books authored by Sirshree, login to:

www.gethappythoughts.org

For further details, call: +91 9011013210

SELECT BOOKS AUTHORED BY SIRSHREE

   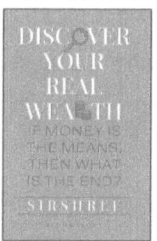

To order these and other books authored by Sirshree
Visit **www.gethappythoughts.org**

Tej Gyan Foundation – Contact details

Registered Office:
Happy Thoughts Building, Vikrant Complex, Near Tapovan Mandir, Pimpri, Pune 411017, INDIA. Contact: +91 20-27411240, +91 20-27412576

MaNaN Ashram:
Survey No. 43, Sanas Nagar, Nandoshi Gaon, Kirkatwadi Phata, Off Sinhagad Road, Taluka Haveli, Pune district - 411024, INDIA. Contact: +91 992100 8060.

WORLD PEACE PRAYER

Divine Light of Love, Bliss, and Peace is Showering;

The Golden Light of Higher Consciousness is Rising;

All negativity on Earth is Dissolving;

Everyone is in Peace and Blissfully Shining;

O God, Gratitude for Everything!

Members of Tej Gyan Foundation have been offering this impersonal mass prayer for many years. Those who are happy can offer this prayer. Those feeling low or suffering from illness can receive healing with this prayer.

If you are feeling troubled or sick, please sit to receive the healing effect of this prayer. Visualize that the divine white healing light is being showered on earth through the prayers of thousands and is also reaching you, bringing you peace and good health. You can dwell in this feeling for some time and then offer your gratitude to those offering the prayer.

A Humble Appeal

More than a million peace lovers are praying for World Peace and Global Healing every morning and evening at 9:09. This prayer is also webcast on YouTube at 9:00 pm. Please participate in this noble endeavor.